BEDTIME STORIES
FOR KIDS

A Collection of Short Tales to Help Children Fall Asleep Fast, and to Feel Calm and Relaxed with Beautiful Dreams

By

SYLVIA LEGHORN

Disclaimer Notice

Please note that the information contained in this document is for educational and entertainment purposes only. The writer made a lot of effort to present accurate, up-to-date, reliable, and complete information. No warranties of any kind are declared or implied. Readers acknowledge that the author is not engaging in the rendering of legal, financial, medical, or professional advice. The author gathered the content of this book from various sources. Please consult a licensed professional before attempting any techniques outlined in this book.

By reading this document, the reader agrees that under no circumstances is the author responsible for any losses, direct or indirect, which might be incurred as a result of the use of the information contained in this document, including, but not limited to, errors, omissions, or inaccuracies.

Copyright © 2021 - All rights reserved.

The content of this book may not be reproduced, duplicated, or transmitted without direct written permission from the author or the publisher.

Under no circumstances will any blame or legal responsibility be held against the publisher, or author, for any damages, reparation, or monetary loss due to the information contained in this book, either directly or indirectly. You are, therefore, responsible for your own choices, actions, and results.

Table of Contents

Introduction 9

What Is A Bedtime Story? 12

    Benefits of Bedtime Stories 12

The Beautiful Christmas Star 15

The Stars in the Sky 19

Seek The Stars And You Will Find Them 27

The Wizard's Pet Mouse 41

Bobo's Castle 43

The Disobedient Lamb And The Wolf 45

The Mystical Moon And The Star 48

The Owl Makes Friends With The Wizard 51

Yuri And The Little Wizard 54

Harry's Magical Pirate Ship 62

- The Sad Starfish 69
- The Wizard 75
- Betty The Secret Princess 87
- Lottie And The Fabulous Whale 92
- The Wizard That Overlooked 95
- The Teddy Bear 101
- A Penguin, A Dark Egg, And An Island 107
- The Magical Unicorn 112
- The Valiant Princess 115
- The Princess And The Dragon 119
- The Greedy Dog 132
- The Princess And The Faithful Knight 134
- Lisa Prepares A Cake 138
- The Lion And The Camel And The Jackal And The Crow 151
- Max Goes For A Walk 157
- The Princess And The Frog 165
- The Bear Feast 171

The Bear And The Travelers 176

David Goes To See The Whales 178

Deer In The Wood 191

In A Rabbit Hole 204

The Duckling Story 211

Tina Feels Sad 219

The Mathematician Prince 231

The Mouse Finds A Snack 236

Conclusion 245

Introduction

I want to thank and congratulate you for reading this book, "**Bedtime stories for kids**."

Welcome to the beautiful world of stories and its magical possibilities. There are various ways to meditate, like by sitting in silence, doing breathing exercises or visualization techniques, and even while walking.

In this whimsical book, you will find many beautiful stories to help your kid nod off each night. Plus, you'll explore incredible new skills that you can use to relax their body so that they sleep soundly all night long.

Before we start with the stories, I would like to discuss the necessity of having a bedtime routine.

Do you have a bedtime routine?

A bedtime routine is what you do every night to help you prepare for going to sleep, so that once you crawl into bed each night you recognize that you are ready for a sweet sleep. Having a good bedtime routine helps you ensure that you're not getting going to end up feeling distracted by your thoughts once you get into bed. This way, you can recognize that you are entirely ready for bed, so that you'll relax, read your story, and then nod off.

Everybody's bedtime routine is different, but you should always include brushing your teeth and putting on a comfy pair of pajamas. You can even sip water, make sure your bed is cozy for you to get into, and grab your favorite stuffed animal so that you've got someone comfy to sleep next to.

Don't forget to say goodnight to your family, too!

Once you've finished your bedtime routine and you're sure that you can nod off, you'll pick a bedtime story and start relaxing. Make sure you read each story and follow along so you have a warm, cozy and honest night's rest. This is essential because it will assist you in being refreshed and prepared for a new day! So, are you ready to help your kid start their bedtime meditation?

Just choose a story to get started!

What Is A Bedtime Story?

Many parents face the challenge of putting their kids to sleep around bedtime, and typically it takes an hour or more to end this daily battle. A practical solution to this problem is to introduce a bedtime routine to your kids. Building a set of habits at bedtime creates security and reliability in their minds, which helps them to feel more relaxed when going to sleep. A simple way of finishing your kids' bedtime routine is by reading them a bedtime story. But why is this so important for your kids?

Benefits of Bedtime Stories

Here are four benefits from reading your kid's bedtime stories:

- Relaxation: Your child will tend to lie still when listening to a story at bedtime. This type of peace will quickly make him/her sleepy.

- Peaceful: A sure way to rest with your child is through reading together with him/her.
- Bonding: Sharing an engaging bedtime story in the warmth of your child's embrace helps to make better bonding.
- Future success: Reading or listening to bedtime stories supports your child's intellectual development. It's an essential element for their future academic success.

Reading books is an excellent way to help your kids to relax and prepare them for sleep. What would happen if your child asked you to stay up reading books upon books? Well, you would be tired and likely doze off a few times, but of course you do not want to disappoint them since they enjoy their books so much, do you? A method to overcome this is to limit the number of books or the length of reading time. When you have reached the limit, you'll tell them it's time for the lights to go out and play an audiobook for your kids after you switch off the light. Playing a story recording in the dark will keep them happy and help them get sleepy faster.

It is vital to consider the type of stories used for ending your bedtime routine, regardless of whether they are bedtime storybooks or bedtime story audiobooks. They ought to be soothing, loving, or relaxing as this can help to make your kids feel calm. It would help if you avoided books that are too exciting, scary, or disturbing. Otherwise, they would keep your kids awake or cause a nightmare, which is not the purpose of reading a bedtime story to them.

The Beautiful Christmas Star

Of the massive number of Stars in the sky, there was one brighter and more beautiful than all of the others. The whole sky's Planets and Stars looked on in reverence, wondering what might have been the important job that this Star did. What's more, the Star itself did the same, mindful of its exceptional beauty. The guessing ended when a gathering of Holy Messengers visited the Star:

"Quick! The time has come; the Lord has requested for you to try and do a crucial job."

So, the Star went as fast as she could and discovered that her job was to point out where the most important event in history would take place.

The Star stood proudly wearing her most beautiful ensemble of sparkle and wonder. She continued to follow the Holy Messengers, who would show her the right spot. The Star shone with such perfection and splendor that everyone could see her from anywhere on the planet. So, a gathering of men chose to follow her, realizing that she must point to something meaningful.

For some time, the Star followed the Holy Messengers who showed the way, she was excited to find the place she would illuminate. Finally, the Holy Messengers stopped, and with incredible happiness, said, "Here it is!" The Star could barely handle what she saw, there were no castles, no strongholds or chateaus, no gold or gems—just a little weakened, filthy, smelly stable.

"Goodness, no! Not that! I cannot squander my sparkle and wonder, illuminating this spot! I was meant for something greater than this!"

Though the Holy Messengers attempted to quiet her, the Star's anger grew and grew. So much pride and egotism rose inside her, and she began to implode. Suddenly, she expanded herself and vanished.

Indeed, what a problem! There was just a few days left before the significant event, and they were without a star. In a frenzy of excitement, the Holy Messengers hurried to Heaven to explain to God what had happened. God thought for a second and then said:

"Look for the littlest, most modest, and joyful of the Stars you can find, and bring it here."

Astonished at the request, yet unquestioning, because the Lord regularly did this type of thing, the Holy Messengers flew through the sky, trying to find the littlest, most joyful Star. They found a modest start. He was so tiny that he gave no significance to his splendor, and he invested all of his energy laughing and talking together with his friends, the best Stars. When they delivered this Star to the Lord, he told him:

"The best and the most splendid Star has exploded due to her pride. I assumed that you, being the most modest and joyful of the various Stars, should be the chosen one to take her spot and light up the most important event ever: the birth of baby Jesus in Bethlehem."

The Star was filled with such a lot of joy and delight that he had been chosen to shine over Bethlehem, until he realised that his brilliance wasn't all that sparkling, he was unable to shine any more than a firefly could.

"Oh," he said to himself. "Why didn't I think about that before taking this job? I'm the smallest Star there is! It's going to be very difficult for me to be the brightest Star in the universe...

It's a disgrace! Ruining a chance that each one of the Stars in the sky would have wanted to have ..."

Then, he thought again, "All the Stars in the sky." They would love to take part in something like this! Then, he decided to go back to the skies with a message for each of his friends:

"On December 25th, in the dark, I want to ask all of you to close your eyes and help to illuminate the introduction of Jesus! You will illuminate the road that leads to the small stable in Bethlehem." None of the Stars dismissed this offer. Such a significant number of Stars came together to shape the most beautiful Star of Christmas that had ever been seen. Who couldn't see the little Star in the whole splendor? Proud of his extraordinary help, and as a reward for his modesty, God turned the little Star into a gorgeous shooting Star and gave him the gift of granting wishes whenever someone saw his beautiful path shining in the night sky.

The Stars in the Sky

Quite a while ago, there was a little Girl who needed to touch the stars in the sky. On clear, moonless evenings, she would lean out of her window, looking up at the thousands of tiny lights opened up across the sky, brooding about what they felt like and wishing to touch them.

On one warm summer evening, a night where the Milky Way sparkled more brilliantly than any time in recent memory, she decided she was unable to take it anymore. She must touch a star or two. So she snuck out of the window and all alone started to find out if she could reach them.

She walked a great distance until she came to a mill wheel, squeaking and crushing ceaselessly.

"Good evening to you," she said to the Mill Wheel. "I want to play with the stars in the sky. Have you ever seen any that are accessible here?"

"Oh, yes," groaned the old Mill Wheel. "They always sparkle in my face from the surface of this pond until I cannot rest. Hop in, my Girl, and you'll discover them."

The Girl jumped into the pond and swam around until she tired out her arms so she could swim no more. Yet, she could not see any stars.

"Pardon me," she called to the old Mill Wheel, "but I do not think there are any stars here at all!"

"Well, before you jumped in and worked the water up, they were there," the Mill Wheel called back. So she got out, dried herself off and began again over the fields.

Soon, she came across a brook, mumbling over its overgrown stones.

"Good evening, Brooklet," she said warmly. "I'm attempting to travel to the stars in the sky so that I can play with them. Have you ever seen any stars nearby here?"

"Oh, yes," murmured the Brooklet. "The stars gleam on my banks around nighttime until I cannot rest. Swim, my child, and you'll find them."

So the Girl swam around a few times and climbed everywhere among the massive rocks; however, not once did she find a star.

"Pardon me," she said as politely as possible, "but I simply don't think there are any stars here."

"What does one mean? No stars here?" the small stream prattled. "There are a lot of stars here. I see them constantly. They spread from the forested area shining right down to the old mill pond on some evenings. There are usually so many that I can't even count them all!" And the Brooklet prattled endlessly until it even forgot the Girl was there. So, she tiptoed away over the fields.

Soon, she sat down to rest in a clearing, and it must have been a pixie knoll because before she knew it, 100 little Pixies were already hastening toward her. They weren't taller than toadstools, yet they were wearing silver and gold.

"Good evening, little folk," said the Girl. "I'm attempting to travel to the stars in the sky. Have you ever seen any stars nearby?"

"Oh, yes," sang the Pixies. "They flicker each night among the cutting edges of the grass. Come and dance with us, female child, and you'll find as many stars as you wish."

So the Girl moved and danced, she spun around in a ring with the small folk, but while the grass shined underneath her feet, she never saw one star. At last, she could dance no more, and she fell inside the ring of Pixies.

"I've tried, and I have tried; but I cannot get to the stars down here," she cried. "If you do not help me, I'll never find any stars to play with."

The fairies all murmured together. At long last, one of them crawled up and took her by the hand and said: "If you're truly determined, you ought to plow ahead. Go straight, make sure that you are on the right street. Request that Four Feet take you to No Feet and afterward tell No Feet to take you to the stairs Without Steps and if you climb that...""Then, I will be among the stars in the sky?" cried the girl.

"If you're not there at that time, you will be elsewhere, won't you?" snickered the fairy, and he disappeared.

So the girl began again with a light heart, and eventually, she visited an outfitted pony tied to a tree.

"Good evening," she said. "I'm trying to get to the stars in the sky. I have come this far, and my bones are throbbing.

Will you give me a ride?"

"I am ignorant of stars in the sky," the pony answered. "I'm here just to give the offering of the small folk."

"Well, I came from the small folk," she cried, "and they said to ask Four Feet to take me to No Feet."

"Four Feet? That's me!" the pony whinnied. "Hop on and ride with me."

They rode all day until they came out of the woodland and stopped at the mouth of the ocean. "I've carried you as far as I can on land, which is how far I can go," said the pony. "Now, I should return home to my people."

So the Girl slid down and walked along the ocean, brooding about what she would do next, until out of nowhere, the most beautiful Fish she'd ever seen appeared.

"Good evening," she said to the Fish. "I'm trying to get to the stars in the sky. Would you be able to help me?" "I'm afraid I cannot," sputtered the Fish, "unless you bring word from the small folk."

"Well, I do," she cried. "They said Four Feet would carry me to No Feet, and afterward, No Feet would take me to the Stairs Without Steps."

"Oh, well," said the Fish, "that's okay then, hop on my back and hang on tightly."

Then, off he went into the water, swimming along a silver path that shimmered and seemed to reach the top of the ocean, where the water met the sky. The Girl saw a gorgeous rainbow emerging from the ocean and into the atmosphere. It was delightful to look at sparkling with all the hues of the world, blues and reds, and greens. The closer they drew, the brighter it sparkled until she needed to hide her eyes from its light.

Finally, they visited the foot, and she saw the rainbow was an expansive brilliant road, inclining far up into the clouds in the sky. At the far end of it, she could see small sparkling things moving around.

"I can go no further," the Fish said. "Here are the Stairs Without Steps. Move up them, however, hang on tight. These steps are not made for the feet of a small Girl, you know." The Girl then jumped off from No Feet, and off he sparkled through the water.

She climbed and moved up to the rainbow. It was not easy. Whenever she made one stride, she seemed to slide back two, and albeit she moved until the ocean was far underneath, the stars in the sky looked further away than they ever had.

"In any case, I won't surrender," she told herself. "I've overcome so much. I cannot return."

Up and up she went. The air grew colder and colder; however, the sky turned brighter and brighter. Finally, she could tell she was approaching the stars.

"I'm nearly there!" she cried.

Then, suddenly, she reached the very top of the rainbow. Wherever she looked, the stars were turning and moving.

They darted here and there, and backwards and forward, and spun in a thousand hues around her.

"I'm finally here," she murmured to herself. She had never seen anything so beautiful that she stood for a few moments in awe of the sky.

But soon, she realized she was shuddering with cold. When she looked down into the dark, she could not see the world. She wondered where her house was, so far away; however, no streetlights or window lights penetrated the darkness below. She began to feel somewhat dizzy.

"I won't go until I touch one star," she told herself and stayed on her toes and extended her arms as high as she could. She went further and further, and suddenly, a falling star sped by and surprised her so much that she lost her balance.

She slid down, down-down-down the rainbow; the further she slid, the warmer it grew, and the warmer it became, consequently, the sleepier she felt. She gave a great yawn and a little sigh, and before she knew it, she was sleeping soundly.

When she awakened, she was in her bed. The sun was peeking through her window, and the morning birds were singing among the brambles and trees.

"Did I touch the stars?" she asked herself, "Or was it just a dream?"

Then, she felt something in her grasp. And when she opened her clenched hand, a little light flashed in her palm and was immediately gone, she smiled because she knew it had been a bit of stardust.

Seek The Stars And You Will Find Them

"I want to see them," Sisi said to her Mother, "now."

She was seven, a young Venezuelan before the time of Bolivar, and, as children frequently seem to be, she was unafraid to dream.

"Well, Sisi," said her Mother as she guided the youthful girl outside, "The stars are right here for you to see.

See?"

Mother was correct. The stars dazzled in the night sky, flashing and sparkling brilliantly like a young child's eye. "No, Mother," Sisi demanded, "I don't only want to see the stars — I would like to feel them up there. I would like to travel to the stars. I would like to touch them."

"Well," said Sisi's Mother, intrigued, amazed and not going to ruin her little girl's dream, "you'll need a path up. The best way to get to that level is with a stepping stool."

"Well, Mother," Sisi asked, "Where will I find a stepping stool?"

"Sisi," her Mother stated, "Stepping stools are everywhere, but none are going to be tall enough."

"Well," Sisi stated, "Where can I find one that is?"

Her Mother sighed. "Sisi, there's not a stepping stool in this great big world sufficiently tall enough for you to touch the stars."

Sisi was momentarily hindered, and, as children frequently do, she tried reaching for her imagination again. "Well, Mother!" she said, as unassumingly as she could, "Then I assume I can make a stepping stool, and it'll take me there."

Her Mother dared not lower her little girl's will, so she made her a promise, "If this is what you would like, then I will be able to bring you wood."

Sisi smiled. She stared up at the stars and drifted off to sleep.

The next day, Sisi was ready to try, and her Mother brought some wood as promised. Sisi was youthful and inexperienced with tools. However, the nearby skilled workers saw her using her hammer as they walked by. They taught her how to carry out her work with wood and nails.

Sisi worked on her project to reach the stars with wood, a hammer, and a ceaseless eagerness.

Every day that passed, with each log her Mother found, Sisi kept on building. Each morning, she would move to the next step with her hammer and nails, she progressed forward and upward.

Days advanced, and seasons passed, and her stepping stool grew ever-taller. She could now look over her home and felt great pride.

"I'm getting closer, Mother!" Sisi yelled from the skies above.

"I know," her Mother stated as she smiled as wide as the crescent moon.

Years passed. Sisi grew. Tall and delightful, she was. The youthful woodworker with the brown eyes pulled in much attention from the town's common folk.

"There's the girl with her stepping stool," stated the lads who would travel through the town.

"I wonder where she's going," they'd think. "I wonder if she wants to fly."

Every morning, Sisi would wake with the crows and continue her journey. When the tree outside gave all its wood, her Mother would travel far into the wild to find more.

As Sisi climbed higher each day, her body grew reliable, and her feet became agile. Faster and faster, she would rise.

Each night, at the last of the sunshine, Sisi would stare off into the skyline, watching the sun together with her eyes. "Someday," Sisi stated, "I will stay up here in the dark. And, I will be able to watch the stars until the first morning light." She knew they'd be as stunning as she dreamed.

Sisi was very fashionable. A person named Santiago venerated her impossible dream, and sometimes in the dark, he would wait for Sisi at the bottom.

Sisi would return home drained and exhausted from each day of climbing and building, and Santiago would give her water from his well and a few fleeces to keep her warm.

"I'm astonished by you," Santiago stated, "You're as intense as you are courageous. I do not know why you are going, but I do know you'll see the stars."

Her Mother used to watch from the window as the two would talk among the owls. Her Mother's smile lit the pieces of her spirit that the moon's light would never reach.

"Santiago," Sisi said one night, tired but with great satisfaction, "My heart can't thank you enough for what you're doing and who you are. You're welcome to stay if you would like."

Santiago's smile produced light in the night, and his heart ran with the horses. He leaned in to let her head lay on his shoulder — and Santiago stayed.

Still, Sisi woke with the crows, waking the sun up every morning. She bid Santiago goodbye and kissed her Mother to say hello. She climbed over the tallest trees to stare out over the mountains and take in the view.

Another step taken, another meter covered, another day closer to the stars.

One day, Sisi rested. She required rest; she really did. For the time had come for Sisi to possess a girl of her own. "I think I will be able to call her Stella," Sisi said to Santiago, radiating proudly and energetically. "It means 'star,' you know." "I know she's beautiful, like you," said Santiago, while Sisi's Mother sobbed in delight.

Years kept on going as Sisi's stepping stool kept on growing. What's more, Stella grew, as well.

Every morning, Sisi rose and kissed Santiago goodbye, kissed her little Stella, and kissed her Mother hello. She climbed the stepping stool with wood from her Mother. She hammered enthusiastically for as long as there was light.

One morning, Sisi rose and bid Santiago goodbye and kissed her little Stella when her Mother created a commotion.

"I'm heartbroken," her Mother stated, "Because finally, there's no wood."

Day or night, her Mother always found Sisi wood for all of these years.

"Is the timberland out of trees?" she asked.

"No," her mother replied. "As I gathered wood for you, I planted seeds. So at some point, they'll become trees."

Sisi gave her Mother another kiss and a warm hug, and at this point, she couldn't let her go. "I think I'll stay here with you, Mother."

Her Mother, weak from years of slashing and scouring and from the procession of her time, lay in Sisi's arms. Sisi brushed her Mother's hair and murmured:

"Without you, I would not be the lady I am today. You showed me how to see the stars and touch them, and as I made a stool you provided me with all that I needed. You never questioned me — you not even once told me to stop. But now, I'm wondering if I should have invested more energy with you, if maybe I shouldn't have left every morning, or have constructed that stepping stool."

"Don't be silly," her old Mother said, gathering herself, "Every morning as you left me, I always knew I was loved.

You'd kiss me and say 'thank you' and provide me gifts from above. Your stepping stool is your greatest gift, for which I'm happy. You always came home; you always remembered who you are and where you came from, no matter what great heights you had reached."

"But, Mother," Sisi stammered, "Will I ever reach the stars?"

"You will," her Mother sighed. Sisi didn't build her stepping stool that day. The news travelled quickly around the town of Sisi's Mother's passing and an excellent parade and feast was held in her memory.

Sisi would lay awake and stress, "Where will I find wood?" She could ask Santiago, however, who would stay with Stella? Sisi pondered, meandered, and attempted to seek out the wood herself, but she knew that to slash, and hammer would drain her time and energy.

She went to bed, grief-stricken, sad, with a broken heart. That night, she didn't dream.

Sisi arose with the crows, kissed her little Stella and Santiago, then wandered outside to think and couldn't believe what she saw.

A pile of wood extending as far as the eye could see appeared before her eyes. An illusion? A miracle? How? Why?

A neighborhood Worker drew closer to Sisi and said:

"Sisi, we've watched you consistently until you rose out of our sight. You climbed this stepping stool, using the wood available and a hammer, and as we've watched, you've reached your dreams." The Worker continued:

"Your Mother passed us by on her way through town and told us where she was going. She said she'd spared a couple of seeds from trees she'd chopped down for you and planted them to become trees one day.

There are miles of trees that stretch over the sunshine. She called your stepping stool 'Amazing,' so she named the woodland 'Amazon.' Once we heard about your Mother, we all got together and decided to plant trees, as we cannot allow you to fail at something you've worked for your entire life to create."

Restored, rededicated, revived, Sisi informed Santiago. "It's a miracle!" she cried.

"It's quite a miracle," said Santiago. "It's your Mother."

Sisi took her hammer and a few planks of wood and then began her morning climb. Stella smiled, and waves of happiness flooded over the citizens.

As Sisi became skilled and her stepping stool grew taller, she could see over the Andes and out over the skyline. "The Pacific was as blue as the relentless sky itself," Sisi thought. "I revere this view. Maybe I don't have to continue anymore."

Be that as it may, Sisi made a vow to her mother that she would meet her in the stars as the rain battered and doused her stepping stool. The breeze whipped her wood and her face; Sisi stood tall and proceeded together with her ascension.

One morning, Sisi rose with the sun and kissed Santiago. She was amazed to find Stella awake.

"Mother," said Stella, "You leave here every morning to create your stepping stool to the stars. Why?" Sisi replied, "It's what I was destined to do."

"Mom," Stella stated, "one day I want to travel to the stars, as well. Will I be able to accompany you?"

"You may," said Sisi, "but you are going to need a hammer, and you'll need to learn how to climb."

That morning, Sisi showed Stella the easier way to carry wood up over the mountains, and the way to pound nails sturdy and thoroughly, and the way to man oeuvre with fast, agile feet and not to fall or lose time.

It went on like this for a time, Sisi and Stella, rising with the crows, rising into the sky, pounding nails into wood, and returning home around nighttime. They giggled and smiled, and Stella learned how to shield herself from the cold wind's blow and, therefore, the determined assault of the rain.

Seasons never stop and consistently show up on time. Winter turned to spring, and spring turned to summer, summer turned to fall. Sisi and Stella kept on building into the sky until:

"Mom! Look! A cloud!" Stella said. "We made it!"

"Go on, Stella, touch it!" Sisi said to her female child. "You have worked hard to reach here. You need to take the lead from here."

So, Stella reached and touched the cloud. It was delicate like silk and soft like a pillow. Sisi nailed the last crossbar into the previous step and utilized a metal snare to append her stepping stool to the cloud where it could rest.

"Mom!" Stella yelled, invigorated with charm. "Are we ready to climb it?"

"Of course, we may!" Sisi said with delight. What's more, Sisi and Stella held hands as they climbed the final steps on their way into the mists. They ran around the cloud; they moved around and relaxed in the heavenly sparkle of the sun. They wrapped themselves in cloud dust. They looked down over the over the tip of the mountain.

As Sisi looked down over every creation, down at the earth beneath her; the Andes, the Amazon, the Venezuelan open country, and her Mother's old home, she thought of Santiago.

"Please," Sisi said to Stella, "It's time for us to travel."

"But Mama!" Stella said to Sisi, "Don't you like to see the stars?"

"My place is down below," said Sisi to Stella. "I'm not able to see them yet."

So Sisi and Stella moved down Sisi's stepping stool to the stars and saw their home rejoin Santiago. "It's done," said Sisi. "My life's work is now finished." And she kissed Santiago, and they hugged. Sisi never expected to release Santiago.

Santiago, brushing the long earthy colored locks of Sisi's hair far away from her breeze whipped face, murmured to her Sisi, "You can stay here for as long as you want, even forever if you wish."

Sisi replied, "That sounds nice. I think I'll do it."

At some point in the future, after Stella had grown into a gorgeous lady and Santiago had become a recognized town elder, Sisi formed a perfect smile.

"The time has come," she said, and she asked Santiago a favor. "If it isn't going to cause you much trouble, gather the townspeople, the specialists, and even the vagabonds here today. I have something very important to tell them." At sunset, in the winter's fresh air, the common folk, dignitaries, and representatives gathered at Sisi's home. After they had all settled down, Sisi rose to speak.

"As you almost certainly are aware," Sisi stated, "This began as a fantasy quite a long time ago when I told my Mother that I needed to observe the stars. Since there was no way for me to climb that high, I decided to seek out how. This stepping stool to the stars has been completed, and today, it will be launched." The townspeople breathed in expectation.

"I wish to open this stepping stool to each one of you, to seek out your way into the mist..." The common folk were thrilled, while the dignitaries were stunned.

"It's you who helped me assemble this with the wood that you found. Although it had been my hands, it had also been yours that helped me. Although it had been my confidence, it had been yours that trusted in me. Although it had been my will, it had been yours that helped me. Though it had been my stepping stool, it had been you that carried me."

The townspeople began to climb. The stepping stool remained fixed. It was made with wood that originated from adoration, nails produced from desire, and an idea created using confidence. Individuals came from great distances worldwide to climb Sisi's stepping stool and take an everlasting look at the stars.

Sisi smiled from down underneath and remained with Stella and Santiago, with a smile as wide as a half-moon, one that lit the night sky and guided the climber's home.

It stayed like this for a short time until Sisi was too weak even to think about smiling. One night, Stella came home to seek her Mother lying in bed, every breath a laborious pant.

"Mother," said Stella. "You can't go yet. You never made it to the stars."

"I know," Sisi stated, brushing locks of Stella's long earthy colored hair far away from her dim face, "I wasn't yet ready — my place was here."

Sisi went on delicately:

"I began building that stepping stool because I wanted to see the stars.

But then, I had you and named you 'Stella' because you were my star.

When your grandmother passed on, she revealed to me that the stars were the place where I'd find her.

Each time I look at you, I see a resemblance of her.

When I started building this stepping stool, I made it for you, but we finally built this together so that you wouldn't have to do it alone.

We finished building it together so that the stepping stool would be our own. Then, you'll always find me when you get your chance to see the stars."

Stella sobbed as Sisi shut her eyes. Then Sisi breathed and eventually saw the stars.

The Wizard's Pet Mouse

A long time ago, there was a magnificent Wizard. One day, he was walking through the village when suddenly a Mouse tumbled to the ground from the beak of a Crow. The Wizard picked up the Mouse and gave him some rice. Later, the Wizard saw a Cat chasing the Mouse around the village. Worried that the Cat would kill his pet Mouse, he transformed the Mouse into a Cat in the hope that it would protect itself.

The following day, the Wizard saw his Cat scared by a Tiger and quickly transformed him into a Tiger to protect himself.

The villagers said, "That isn't a Tiger! It's only a Mouse that the Wizard turned into a Tiger. He can't eat us or scare us."

When the Tiger heard this, he was angry with the Wizard. He thought, 'As long as the Wizard is alive, everyone will know that I'm a mouse!'

When the Wizard saw the Tiger coming, he cast his spell and yelled, "Get back to the shape of a Mouse." The Tiger shrank and turned back to a little Mouse.

Bobo's Castle

The castle sat on a tall mountain and looked like it was trying to touch the sky. It was a dark and sad castle, and in it lived the Wizard, Bobo. Who hated it.

He wished it had been a beautiful and alluring castle, one that might not scare everybody away. He had no friends because they were all frightened of where he lived.

When he was walking in the town one day, a couple of little Kids came to him and said, "Wizard Bobo, we would like to be your friends, but we do not like your castle."

"I don't like it either," the Wizard said sadly. "But what is to be done?"

"You could paint it."

"You could plant flowers all around it."

"You could open the windows and let the sun in."

He considered all of the recommendations then gestured happily. "Yes, I will be able to do all of that, thank you, children! Can you visit me once I am done?" "Oh, yes, we will!" they said together.

So Wizard Bobo departed to his castle. He stood before it and considered what he should do. When he decided, he waved his magic wand and said a few magic words, then he looked in awe at what he had created. A shining white castle with blue windows and doors now stood before him. Flowers grew up and down the walls and straight up to the front entrance. The sun shone splendidly on the new paint, and birds and butterflies flew around it. Wizard Bobo now felt more joyful and much more splendid, and he immediately went inside to inspect it. Lively hues showed abreast of the walls, and he was delighted. Breezes blew in through the open windows, birds sang outside, and the sun peeped in merrily.

He walked back to the town to tell the Kids to come to his beautiful castle.

The Disobedient Lamb And The Wolf

Once, there was a naughty Sheep whose Mother adored him as a child and was always protective of him. His Mother cautioned him, "Be careful! You must not enter the forest. Wild creatures live there. They'll threaten you. A number of them would even eat you." But the naughty Sheep never listened and always stubbornly went into the forest to play until it got dark.

One day, as usual, the Sheep wandered far into the forest. There he saw a spring. "I am thirsty. Let me drink some water," he thought. He chose to drink water from the spring to quench his thirst. While the Sheep was relaxing in the spring, a Wolf watched from behind a tree.

"A Sheep! My lucky day!" the Wolf thought, moving toward the Sheep. The Sheep didn't see the Wolf for quite a while. There was nobody around to save the Sheep from the Wolf.

"You know this forest is a habitat for wild creatures like me. Why do you always come here to use water from this spring?" asked the Wolf.

The Sheep knew that wolves were dangerous creatures. "Mother has cautioned me about wolves. I'm certain this one wants to eat me for his lunch. This Wolf is savage. I need to get away from this creature," he thought.

The Wolf continued, "You have messed up the water. How will I drink this polluted water now?"

"But the spring streams from where you're standing right down to where I'm standing, Sir!" said the Sheep, in a cautious voice. The Wolf was astounded to listen to such an intelligent answer from the Sheep. But the Wolf was looking for a reason to kill the sheep. "How could you try and deal with me? I'm sure you're the same Sheep who mistreated me last year," the Wolf shouted.

"Last year? Goodness Sir, I wasn't even born then!" the Sheep squeaked. The sheep expected that the Wolf was trying to find a reason to kill him. The Sheep became cautious of his words and gestures. It meant that both the Sheep and the Wolf talked to each other cautiously.

The Sheep heard a couple of Lumberjacks. They were coming down the path where the Sheep and the Wolf were standing.

"If I can lecture this Wolf for a little while longer, the Lumberjacks are going to be here. They're going to chase him away," thought the small Sheep. So, he said, "Mr. Wolf, you're right. I have messed up the water. But, I didn't mean to upset you."

The Sheep kept on talking until the lumberjacks showed up. They saw both the Sheep and the Wolf.

They caught the Wolf and beat him before letting him go. The Lumberjacks led the Sheep back to his shelter. He ran back to his Mother, told her what had happened in the forest with a Wolf and the Lumberjacks. And then, he promised his Mother that he would never wander into the woods again.

The Mystical Moon And The Star

One night, high in the dark midnight sky, the Moon was cheerfully watching her children, the Stars playing. One of the Stars was sitting without anyone else and not sparkling as splendidly because of the other Stars.

"What's the matter, little one? Why aren't you playing with the other Stars? And why are you so miserable?" the Moon asked.

"Mother, what happens to us once you send us away?" asked the Star with a bit of a whine.

The Moon smiled at the Star as some of the other Stars heard the inquiry and gathered around. "Yes, Mother, what happens to us after you've sent us away?" another Star asked.

"Please let us know," said another.

The Moon glanced at her children: "When you're old enough, and your lights are beginning to fade, I send you to Earth so that you'll start your next life. Then, you become a part of the world," she said, pointing to the world underneath her, she continued, "some of you will be trees and plants, some will be animals, and others will be the folks that live and respect us from far away. Finally, when your time on Earth is complete, you'll be sent back to me."

All the Stars smiled and began to think about the things they would like to become. However, despite everything, the little Star seemed to be miserable: "What if we don't want to leave?" asked the little Star.

"Is there an honest reason why you would not have any desire to go away, little one?" asked the Moon.

"I'm on the verge of leaving, but I do not know if I'm prepared to go away yet," said the Star, looking down on Earth. The Moon responded, "One day, you'll return to me and so will the other Stars, and you'll have lots of stories about the things you saw down there."

The little Star loved the thought of returning and having a story to tell and smiled, "Well, when you put it that way," it said.

"I can hardly wait till I'm down there," the Star shouted.

The Moon smiled and sent the little Star down, watching it shine bright as it moved toward the world. Different Stars smiled and watched the little Star, pondering what it would be like to be on Earth. The life pattern of the Stars continued in this manner. The Moon would send her children down when their lives as Stars had finished and watched over them consistently, watching what things they did and the people they saw until it was time for them to meet her again as a Star. She would smile when her children would tell her stories of what they did while they lived on Earth. Thus, on went the cycle, the Stars travelling every time telling the Moon their stories, starting with one life then onto another.

The Owl Makes Friends With The Wizard

Although many wizards lived in his time, Odin was a very talented wizard. But still, it had taken him a lifetime of experience to reach where he was today, not to mention he was a zillion years old. Odin was very famous. He was a gorgeous, magical character filled with vitality and fun, capable of changing himself into many personalities. One of his favorites was the Owl, filled with knowledge and prepared to seek out anything in the dark of night.

He was everywhere and nowhere, but also, here and there.

This famous wizard had the skill of being anywhere and at any time, to such an extent that everyone knew he was always near and therefore they felt safe.

He had a steady partner, a wise old Owl who had been with him for as long as anyone could remember.

You could hear the Owl hooting' and know that Odin was someplace close.

On one particular evening, Odin was sitting on a tree branch with the Owl. He was brooding about a wish that he had been carrying with him for a very long time. No matter how much he tried with all his magical forces to make it come true, it just wouldn't. Odin had known the mysteries of life for a long time and what to do, and the way to understand things quickly. What's more, everything had been easy for him.

Well, he'd say. "That is what all wizards do… right?"

Yes, but everyone can do this thing, even the other wizards; he hoped that they might have the chance to use all of the knowledge in the universe. However, how would he do this? He had tried numerous ways.

"Oh, well," he thought.

"At some point or another, it'll come to me. It's no use trying to force it, eh, Owl?"

To which Owl only "hooted" back to him. "I know, I do know what you're thinking Owl… that I cannot and will not force this stuff… but it makes me so impatient… it truly does."

Just then, a gathering of youngsters came to play. A number of them began to kick a ball around; some were walking about and talking with each other. Others were playing hide and seek.

You could tell how carefree they were, laughing and shouting with one another, without a care in the world. Odin was ready to see their thoughts and to see how happy they were, for their innocence radiated through them.

"Okay," he thought.

"If they might just stay that way, it might be straightforward for them to succeed even inside of himself! And use their hidden information to help themselves and others."

"You know, Owl," he continued, "When one is happy and content with the planet and oneself, the sky is the limit. Don't you agree? What's more, a good range of possibilities exist, considering the information we have at our disposal."

Odin was getting so energized with these thoughts that were tumbling wildly in him that he nearly lost his balance on the branch.

He quickly grabbed a twig nearby to balance himself. Owl jumped and opened his wings out a couple of inches and, together with his wings fluttering, rebalanced himself.

Yuri And The Little Wizard

Once upon a time, there was a gorgeous Sapphire City. It stretched across the fairyland of Fae. A magnificent girl called Princess Yuri was the leader of the state. Among the people that served this Princess and lived in a comfortable suite of rooms in her magnificent castle was a little older man referred to as the Wizard of Sapphires. This tiny Wizard could do many things with magic. And he was a caring man, with bright, sparkling eyes and a sweet smile. So instead of dreading him, due to his charm everyone adored him.

Yuri believed that everyone who occupied the gorgeous Land of Fae should be happy and satisfied. So, she chose one morning to visit all parts of the state, so if she found that anything wasn't suitable, or anybody was disappointed, she would correct it. She requested that the tiny Wizard accompanied her, and he was happy to travel.

"Should I bring my pack of magic tools with me?" he asked.

"Yes," said Yuri. "We may need tons of magic before we return, for we are going into odd corners of the land. We may encounter obscure animals and have dangerous experiences."

So the Wizard took his pack of magic tools and the two left Sapphire City and wandered over the state for an extended time. They finally reached a spot far up in the mountains, which neither of them had ever been to before. Stopping one morning at a cabin, on the brink of the roadway which went through a beautiful valley, Yuri asked a Man:

"Are you happy? Have you any complaint to make about your life?"

The Man answered, "There are three mischievous Imps that sleep in the valley and frequently come here to harass us. If your Highness would just chase away those Imps, my family and I would be very pleased and appreciative to you."

"Who are these awful Imps?" asked the Princess.

"Their names are Olite, Udent, and Ertinent. These Imps have no regard for anybody or anything. If outsiders pass through the valley, the Imps sneer at them, make terrible faces, call them names, and frequently push travelers or toss stones at them. Whenever Imp Olite or Imp Udent or Imp Ertinent come here to bother us, my family, and I run into the house and lock all the doors and windows. We dare not venture out again until the Imps have left."

Princess Yuri was surprised to hear this report, and the little Wizard shook his head gravely and said the nasty Imps had to stop. They told the great man they were ready to do whatever was needed to guard him, and without a moment's delay, they entered the valley to look for the house of the three mischievous Imps.

After a brief time, they came across three caverns, and before each cavern, hunched an eccentric little person. Yuri and the Wizard stopped to examine them and found that they were considerably formed and enthusiastic. They had substantial round ears, long noses, and wide smiling mouths, and their pure black hair came to points on their heads, looking very similar to horns. Their clothes fitted snuggly to their bodies and appendages, and the Imps were so tiny in size that Yuri didn't consider them to be at all dangerous. But one of them suddenly reached out a hand and grabbed the Princess's dress, pulling it so sharply that she almost fell, and after a second, another Imp pushed the small Wizard so forcefully that he knocked against Yuri. Both fell heavily on their bottoms.

In response, the Imps laughed loudly and began running around and kicking dust on the Princess, who cried out in a loud voice: "Wizard, do your job!"

The Wizard jumped into action. Without hesitation, he opened his sack, got the tools he required, and mumbled a spell.

In a flash, the three Imps became three bushes—the prickly kind—with their roots in the ground. The bushes stood still, maybe from shock at their unexpected change. The Wizard and the Princess found time to brush themselves off. Yuri then approached the bushes and said: "The situation you currently suffer, my poor Imps, is merely because of your insidious activities. You'll no longer annoy innocent travelers, and you'll stay as bushes, secured with sharp thorns, unless you apologize for your terrible ways and promise to be good Imps."

"They can't resist being good now, your Highness," said the Wizard, who was very satisfied with his work, "and the safest arrangement would be to make them stay as bushes."

However, something wasn't right with the Wizard's magic, for no sooner had the words came out of his mouth, the bushes began to move. From the surface, they just waved their branches at the Princess and Wizard. However, as soon as they began to glide over the bottom, their roots started pulling through the earth. One launched itself against the Wizard and pricked him so sharply with its thistles that he shouted out: "Ouch!" and tried to escape.

Yuri struggled to move as the surrounding bushes attempted to hurt her with their thorns. Finally, one tore a hole into her beautiful dress. The Princess ran after the Wizard, who was running for safety until he fell headfirst on deadwood. She ran behind a tree and yelled at the Wizard: "Quick! Change them into something else."

The Wizard heard her; however, he was very dizzy from his fall. Grabbing from his pack, the first magical device he could find, he changed the bushes into three white pigs. That surprised the Imps. Looking like pigs—fat, roly-poly, and charming—they rushed off and lay on the ground looking at each other to better understand their current condition.

Yuri drew an extended breath, and coming from behind the tree; she said, "That is far better, Wizard, for such pigs as these must be very innocuous. Nobody must dread the mischievous Imps."

"I wanted to change them into mice," answered the Wizard, "yet in my dizziness, I worked the wrong magic. But, if the animals don't keep the peace from now onwards, they're in danger of being murdered and eaten. They could become cuts of meats or dishes."

However, the Imps were furious and did not expect to carry on as pigs. As Yuri and the little Wizard left to continue their excursion, the three pigs hurried forward, ran between their legs, and tripped them up, and they both lost their balance and toppled over on top of each other. As the Wizard tried to get up, he tripped again and fell over the rear of the third pig, which carried him far down into the valley until it dumped the tiny Wizard in the river. Yuri lay on the ground, but she hadn't been harmed. So she got herself up and hurried to the assistance of the Wizard, grabbing him as he was crawling out of the stream, panting for breath and dripping with water. The Princess couldn't resist laughing at his woeful appearance. But he had no sooner wiped the water from his eyes when one of the naughty pigs tripped him again and sent him back into the stream for an additional bath. The pigs attempted to trip Yuri, but she hid behind a stump to get out of their way. The Wizard climbed out of the water again and found a pointy stick to protect himself. Then, he murmured a spell that immediately dried his clothes, next he rushed to assist Yuri. The pigs feared the sharp stick and moved away from it.

"This won't do," said the Princess. "We have achieved nothing, for the pig Imps will annoy travelers as much as the real Imps. Change them into something different, Wizard."

The Wizard tried to think. Then, he changed the white pigs into three bluebirds.

"Birds are the most harmless things on earth," he said.

But he had barely spoken when the bluebirds flew at them and attempted to peck at their eyes. As they tried to shield their eyes from the unexpected attack from the supposedly harmless birds, two of the bluebirds pecked at the Wizard's fingers. One got the ear of Princess in its beak and gave it such a ferocious peck that she screamed and tossed her skirt over her head. "These flying creatures are more awful than the pigs, Wizard," she said to her friend. "No one is really harmless as long as they are alive, you ought to change the Imps into something that isn't alive." The Wizard was preoccupied with driving off the birds. However, he managed to open his magic pack and find a spell that directly changed the birds into three buttons. As they tumbled to the bottom, he picked them up and smiled with fulfilment. The tin button was Imp Olite, the steel button was Imp Udent, and the lead button was Imp Ertinent. The Wizard put the three buttons in a box, which he then put in his coat pocket.

"Now," he said, "the Imps can't annoy travelers, for we'll bring them back with us to the Sapphire City." "Still, we should never use the buttons," said Yuri, smiling once again since the threat was now gone.

"Why not?" asked the Wizard. "I mean to stitch them upon my jacket and watch them cautiously. The Imps' spirits are still in the buttons, and after a while, they're going to atone and be sorry for their mischief, then they're going to prefer to be good. Once they want to be good, the tin button will change to silver and the steel to gold, while the lead button will become copper. At that time, I will turn them back to their appropriate forms, changing their names to pretty names instead of the revolting ones they used to bear. From then on, the three Imps are going to be good residents of the Land of Fae, and I'm sure you'll find they're going to be loyal subjects of our darling Princess Yuri."

"Oh, that's good magic," shouted Yuri, very satisfied. "There is not any uncertainty here, old flame, you simply are a cunning Wizard."

Harry's Magical Pirate Ship

There was once a little boy called Harry, whose dream was to have his own Pirate ship and sail around the oceans, finding the treasure that was lost a long time ago.

Harry spent the weekend together with his Grandma and Grandpa. His Mother would drop him off each Saturday morning at 9 o'clock on the dot and pick him back up on Sundays at 6 o'clock soon after dinner.

Grandma and Grandpa's home was a large old homestead house with an enormous garden. It was on the brink of a meadow filled with dazzling flowers, and at the bottom of the garden stood Grandpa's workshop and an old shed.

One bright Sunday morning, Harry was sitting at the table together with his Grandpa, eating. He told him that he had a dream last night that he was a Pirate skipper trying to find lost treasure. Grandpa said to little Harry, "Well, to seek out any lost Pirate treasure, you would need a treasure map! Pirates can't go anywhere without a map," So little Harry and his Grandpa spent the whole morning making a map to seek out the lost treasure. There were many perils for Pirates trying to find treasure. Once they had finished, the map showed sharks, a bunker, and other Pirates little Harry would need to defeat.

Harry's Mother showed up to take him home. He hugged his Grandpa goodbye, and off he went, still brooding about Pirates and the lost treasure.

The following day, Harry's Grandpa thought he would start to build Harry's Pirate ship from his dream to surprise him the following weekend. It might take a while, so Grandpa got right to work! Grandpa realized he needed tons of wood to create a wonderful Pirate ship, and searching in the garden, he saw his small shed that had been standing there with just bits of garbage in it for quite a while, "That's it," Grandpa thought to himself "I can use the wood from the old shed."

Grandpa opened the shed door to seek an old car wheel from a car he'd had a few years back. And also, an old chime used to hold the shed door closed. Grandpa thought they might be suitable for the Pirate ship, so he set them aside and began to tug down the old shed. He laid down all the boards of wood on the grass. He then carried them into his workshop, where he would hack the wood and start making little Harry's dream Pirate ship.

Grandpa visited the workshop to build the Pirate ship for the subsequent days. He would get up early every morning and only stopped when Grandma would yell down into the garden, "Your tea is ready!"

Friday soon arrived. It was a showcase day in the town. Grandma always visited the market on a Friday for shopping. Before leaving, Grandma asked Grandpa: "Is there anything you need?"

"Yes," Grandpa answered, "There's a vendor in town that sells flags; if you don't mind, would you be willing to look for an enormous black flag to place on Harry's Pirate ship?"

Off Grandma went to do her shopping with a bag and a list of the items she required.

It took a long time for Grandpa to paint the Pirate ship and fit the old wheel he found in the shed. Grandpa fastened the wheel to the front of the ship. Then, he put the old chime on the back, "I thought the ringer would be useful and give little Harry something to ring if he got into any danger with the Pirates."

Grandpa found some old rope and a few old sheet materials at the rear of his workshop, which he would use to construct a sail for the ship, all that was required now was for Grandma to return with the black flag so he could make it the very best feature of little Harry's Pirate ship.

Saturday morning was the day of the enormous surprise for Harry, and at 9 o'clock on the dot, he came running down the way with a big smile across his face. The first thing Harry said was, "Hi there, Grandma, where is my Grandpa?!"

"He's down in the garden," Grandma answered, "But before you depart, don't I deserve a hug?"

"Oh, sorry, Grandma," said Harry, and he gave his Grandma an enormous hug, and off he raced to seek out his Grandpa.

Grandpa was standing at the front of his workshop when Harry approached him and hugged him. Harry asked, "Have you continued to look for the treasure, Grandpa?"

"I have," answered Grandpa, "and I even have an enormous surprise for you," Grandpa pulled open the large workshop door for Harry to see that he had built his dream Pirate ship! "Amazing!" said little Harry, "Is it mine?" Harry's eyes lit up, and he had the most perfect smile that a little boy could ever have. "Wow, thank you, Grandpa, my dream has come true!"

Grandpa hauled the Pirate ship from the workshop to the hill so that Harry could play. Little Harry went up into the Pirate ship and started leading the way and ringing the ringer to warn other Pirates that he now had his boat and then he set off to get the treasure.

"Did you forget something?" asked Grandpa as he passed Harry the treasure map they had made last weekend.

Grandpa came back to the farmhouse and made some tea. He sat at the table, reading his paper, feeling happy and pleased that he had made Harry's dream Pirate ship.

Harry was on his ship, yelling requests to his crew, when out of nowhere, the grass in the meadow went from green to a gorgeous ocean blue. His boat started bouncing up and down on the waves. "Amazing," thought Harry, "It must be a magic Pirate ship! Now I can truly embark on the journey to find the lost treasure!"

So off Harry sailed on his journey holding the treasure map in one hand and controlling the ship in the other. He had been cruising for quite a while when he spotted what looked to be an island. Harry set his route for the island as he felt it might be the best spot for burying treasure.

After miles and miles of further cruising, Harry, at last, got to the island. It seemed to be much smaller than when he had first spotted it from his Pirate ship adrift. It had been roughly about the dimensions of Grandpa's back garden.

Harry climbed out of his ship, hanging on tight to his map. The map he and his Grandpa had drawn the previous weekend told him what direction to travel, and he started digging after he reached a small tree. He dug one hole and found no treasure, so he tried again a little further along the way. Harry was searching endlessly when he hit something hard out of nowhere. It was a little wooden box. He cleaned the sand off and pulled open the top. Inside the container were packages and many gleaming gold coins. "Yes! I've found the treasure," Harry yelled.

He took the container and went back to his Pirate ship. Little Harry soon realized that he had forgotten to tie the boat to anything when he first got to the island and had been so busy digging; he hadn't seen that his Pirate ship had sailed away.

"Oh no!" thought Harry, "How am I going to get back home to Grandpa and Grandma?"

Harry sat down and started crying. Suddenly, little Harry heard a voice, it was Grandpa's voice, yelling his name. Harry asked, "How did you discover me?"

"You dozed off on your Pirate ship," answered Grandpa, "You were probably dreaming."

Little Harry arose and climbed out of his Pirate ship and began to tell his Grandpa all about the dream on his magical

Pirate ship. "What is that in your pocket Harry?" asked Grandpa, and when Harry checked, he found one gleaming gold coin.

The Sad Starfish

Once upon a time!

In a protected pool of water, amid the rocks at the ocean's edge, there was a little starfish named Stanley. The water was always warm and salty where Stanley lived, and his abode beneath the surface made him very happy.

During the day, Stanley played in the sand that sparkled and shone in the warm sunshine. After the sun slipped below the horizon at night, Stanley would cuddle up on the brink of his favorite rock and fall into a deep sleep.

One day, Stanley saw that although his house was comfortable, something was missing.

It was quiet. Too quiet!

The Starfish was very sad because there was nobody to speak to or play with. This made the small Starfish became very sad.

Stanley considered this throughout the day. When the Sun slipped away that night, he was lonelier than he had ever felt before.

He moved over to his favorite rock and attempted to snuggle down to rest; however, the rock seemed to be excessively hard and excessively cold for reasons unknown.

"If I only had somebody to speak to...." Stanley said to himself. "Then, I would not be so sad."

Stanley looked upward and started to observe the night sky. Individually, splendid, twinkling stars showed up, carrying delicate light to the darkness.

Stanley had never observed the stars. He was usually always sleeping before the moon laid its beauty over the water. This new sight was astounding.

"That's it!" Stanley exclaimed, sitting straight up.

"There is not much room in this little pool. No wonder I'm so sad, I must be a star that fell from the sky! But how will I ever get back up there?"

He could see how the moon covered the good ocean, and he concluded that it must be the way back to the sky. He would find a route that way.

Stanley stayed awake throughout the night, mulling over how he could get to the big bright moon. Stanley had never left his comfortable tiny home. Finally, he concluded that he would, by any means possible, leave the comfort of his small house for the encompassing ocean to get to the stars above the night sky.

When the tide came in the following morning, Stanley climbed into the swirling water. The high waves immediately hurried him away out into the vast ocean.

Stanley rolled and tumbled across the heavy waves and ocean currents. This adventure was mind-blowing. Finally, the twirling and turning stopped, and Stanley drifted gradually down to the ocean's floor.

An old Seahorse watching from a close distance began to laugh.

"Silly little Starfish!" he snickered.

The Starfish had learned in class never to speak with outsiders. "If you would like to understand the moon's way, I will be able to tell you this; you'll only find it in the dark."

Although frustrated, Stanley realized it must be true because he had never seen the moon in the day. Stanley chose to calm down in the sand and trust that night will come. He would take a nap after his restless night.

Stanley had barely dozed off when he heard a peculiar commotion that sounded a lot like someone yelling.

"WAKE UP!"

Stanley opened his eyes. A ravenous monster was swimming right toward him, licking its lips and smiling. Quickly, Stanley ducked into an outsized dark spot under a rock and huddled there, shaking with fear. When a voice came from behind him, he was so scared that he jumped straight up and knocked his head on the rock.

"It's okay now! Calm down," the voice said. "That vast Pufferfish must have frightened you! Golly, don't you realize that a Starfish should never rest in the open that way? You were fortunate, you know! You almost became that big fish's supper! "

Stanley moved in the voice's direction and positioned himself eye to eye with another little Starfish.

"Gracious, many thanks for saving my life," Stanley wheezed. "I had no clue it might be so dangerous over here!" Stanley squinted as he took a glance at the other little Starfish. "But who are you? What's your name? Did you fall from the sky, as well?" Stanley asked enthusiastically. "Maybe we will find our way back together!"

The new little Starfish chuckled, "My name is Marcie. Fall from the sky? What in the world are you talking about?" So Stanley acquainted himself with Marcie and clarified how sad his little pool in the rocks was, with nobody around to speak to or play with. He told her how he had seen the sky so filled with stars and was checking out the moon's path to lead him up to his twinkling family in the sky.

"Gracious, Stanley!" Marcie snickered. "You do not have a place up in the sky! You are a Starfish, like me! Starfish have a place in the water! Anyway, I do not think the moon's way could ever lead you to the sky. The Seahorse told me it's only a mirrored image of the moon, in the water."

Stanley took a glance at Marcie. "Then I assume I should head home," he said, "however, it has been so lonely there." Then, Stanley began to inform his new companion of his peaceful, safe home, the friendly and cozy Sun, sparkling sand, and his favorite rock.

"That sounds awesome!" shouted Marcie. "But why would you ever leave it? The ocean is filled with numerous threats, and the sun barely ever shines on the deep waters."

"You're right," murmured Stanley. "I would prefer not to stick around here. It's icy and unsafe. It's just that I used to be so sad back there without anyone else."

"I have an excellent idea!" said Marcie. "If you wish, I'll return to the rocks by the shore with you. I will be able to stay and be your friend forever. We will talk and play together, and you'll never be lonely again!"

"Will you? Truly? I might like that, Marcie!" Stanley shouted cheerfully. "We'll be best friends! But it'll be high water soon, so we should move quickly if we are to return home!"

Together, Marcie and Stanley moved along toward the ocean's floor, where the tide's swirling waters could bring them closer to shore.

They stayed in close proximity so that they would not lose each other during the dangerous situations, and shortly they tumbled securely back to Stanley's shielded little pool amid the rocks in the water

Stanley happily showed Marcie around his comfortable tiny home. Then, because the sun slipped below the horizon and the stars above began to fill the sky with sparkling splendor, Stanley and Marcie cuddled up to Stanley's favorite rock and, smiling at each other, they both fell asleep.

The Wizard

Somewhere inside an enchanted forest, a butterfly jumped from the branch it had been resting on, fluttered its wings, and started to make its way through the thick undergrowth, turning along leaves and crisscrossing wildly underneath the shade that was its home. After a brief time, the trees began to thin, and the butterfly found itself in a bit of clearing. In this clearing was a frail cabin with a thick, ivy-covered rooftop and a solitary broken window, whose tiny curtains were discolored by dirt and it was hard to imagine they allowed any light to enter at all.

Despite its condition, the house was sturdy and had an oddly strong appearance, which proposed that not everything was as it seemed. As the butterfly bounced calmly past the furthest room of the structure, its shape sparkled and altered for a second, developing into something bigger and truly more fearsome than one would expect. Then, once past the cabin, it took its ordinary shape and continued its excursion into the forest. Had anybody been watching closely, they might have wondered about two things. First, the time taken for the butterfly to cross the cabin's structure seemed to be far longer than was necessary. And also, just for the briefest of seconds, the house appeared to assume the shape of a small post, with blue rock walls and a banner flying from its bulwarks. Inside the house, the darkness won, except for a bright sparkle in the middle of the space. There, lit up from below, a Wizard stood slumped over an oversized wooden table. Moving his gaze away from the cauldron in front of him, he twirled with a sparkle. As he beheld the impossible suspension of changing precious stones and six short columns of wooden glyphs, he thought about the outcome of this dangerous experiment and the devastating effect it might have in the hands of the ignorant. By the side of the magic mixture laid the Wizard's wand, a short, squat stick as old as the bungalow itself, which had, throughout the years, worn itself into a shape that fitted the Wizard's hand. Moving his head as if to diminish the uneasiness of extending his neck over the sizzling cauldron, the Wizard ran a tough hand through his wiry and diminishing hair; the approaching night would be a challenging one, he thought, as he soberly stroked his rough stubbles. Perhaps his most formidable challenge yet. Everybody's most formidable challenge, indeed. He'd heard it before all the times he had fallen into the magical traps of Wizards, Witches, and Sorcerers, while protecting every part of the known world. Everybody had been discussing it. The whole network hummed with gossipy tidbits about the impending attack by the Dark One and the fearsome rebel Enchanter called Hakko.

The Wizard realized that he was only a small part of all those who went against Hacker. Yet, he felt that he was the one in charge of the cabin guard and realized that many others, like himself, felt the same way. Spending the majority of the day updating his spells and charms, he tried looking for Hacker's attack without a clue of what form it might take. As sunset drew near, all he could think of was rest.

Gazing profoundly into the cauldron entranced by the delicately whirling, multi-hued pattern within, the Wizard repeated his spell again and again as if to console himself before the fight started. "My Chi is more grounded than your Chi," he said, the words echoing off the grime-ridden walls. He did not know where or when he had first heard the spell, yet it still held power. Gradually he turned his hands over each other in a mysterious round, clearing movement.

All of a sudden, Hacker's attack began. The whirling hues inside the cauldron abruptly disappeared to get replaced by a uniform of pure black sheen, with one spot of brilliant green in its middle, which immediately grew into a gleaming line of abnormally twisting images. As it did, the Wizard jumped into action, fingers leaving the wooden glyphs quickly on his table as he put up a firewall. Outside, a sheet of fireside thirty feet high showed up in a ring round the bungalow and commenced to flare as Hacker's soldiers tossed themselves powerlessly against it. Inside, the Wizard smiled tiredly to himself. Bots, he thought. Hacker is using bots. What an amateur. Unfortunately, the poor people would continue doing what they are told until they run out of steam or are destroyed by the firewall. They were no danger and indeed not what Hacker typically used. Perhaps he was testing the road, messing around until he began his actual attack.

After a few seconds, another pattern of images showed abreast of the cauldron's face. The Wizard's temples wrinkled as he attempted to decode the pictures, and afterwards, he gestured to himself in acknowledgement, "Crawlers". Around three minutes away and coming quick. Although Crawlers were like Bots, their technique of attack was undeniably more powerful. As when trying to overpower an adversary's protection by the sheer power of numbers, Crawlers would instead meticulously test them, checking out any shortcoming that they might abuse, by actually crawling along the road, as their name proposed. However, thought the Wizard, with an empty, rough laugh, they will discover no openings in his firewall that was for sure. He'd checked the spells multiple times that morning and set the wall in to be impenetrable to the present kind of attack. This meant protection for now, but the Wizard remained alert so that nothing got past. Waving a fork over the ever-quiet glyphs, he produced a reflecting charm. He made a mirrored image of the bungalow, the firewall, and a mile further into the forest. With a few more goes of his hands, he weakened the duplicates' firewall a little, making it a little easier for the approaching Crawlers.

As the Crawlers began to look for their new objective, and the firewall held quickly, the Wizard directed his concentration toward the network. It's good to keep an eye fixed on the others, to make sure that they were okay, he thought. With a quick tap of his wand, the pattern in the cauldron changed, uncovering a map of sorts, with a spider web of lines connecting a progression of disconnected specks. After reading the map for a few seconds, the Wizard shut his eyes and allowed himself to hitch the network. From the beginning, everything he could see was darkness. Then, one figure after another settled themselves before him. Amazingly and alarmingly, some of the faces he had been expecting to see were missing. Malvern, the Dragon Slayer, wasn't there for one. Nor was Pokier Nine, Protector of the North. Without waiting to converse with the others, the Wizard suddenly broke contact and opened his eyes once again. Looking more carefully at the cauldron, he was sure, both Malvern and Pokier's spots had turned a distressing shade of red, which could mean just one thing: that he had penetrated their resistances and that they had fallen. It had been both moronic and a disgrace, he thought, unfortunately, to be beaten by a pack of basic Bots and Crawlers. Neither of them had refreshed spells before the attack, and with Crawlers gone and the magical web debilitated, now, it is up to him and the others to take up the leeway. The Wizard had no chance to grieve the loss of those individual Mages because then, the cauldron's fluid turned a splendid orange. A progression of profoundly disturbing dark images showed abreast of its sleek surface. Accordingly, the Wizard brought his hands to the wooden glyphs in hit or miss succession and put forth a valiant effort to keep off the foremost recent risk, a flood of Spoolers and Worms that had crawled up to him, unnoticed while he'd been communing with others. The Worms were terrible enough. They might tunnel underneath the firewall and attack from in, yet it had been the Spoolers that stressed the Wizard most. He nearly felt the facility of their effect as they came out of the darkness, arms thrashing as they flung bits of themselves against the blazing wall with garbled anger. If they compared the bots to tossing rocks, then the Spoolers would be compared to launching blades - incredibly sharp knives. If they or the worms found out how to move beyond the firewall, then all of his privileged insights would fall to Hacker, who might savagely abuse them to the impediment of the whole network and the world beyond. In anger, the Wizard shouted out: "My Chi is more grounded than your Chi!" and, holding his wand firmly, pounded it down hard onto the table. Accordingly, outside the bungalow, the air turned blue with magic sparkles because the firewall blasted even more brightly. Tongues of white-hot fire burst out from it, incinerating the Spoolers where they stood and heating the Worms into the bottom beneath as they attempted to tunnel underneath.

No sooner had the attack been diverted than the Wizard was quickly distracted by another message floating on the cauldron's surface. Absentmindedly cleaning the sweat from his temple with the sleeve of his robe, he saw who the message was from, then smiled to himself before letting out another rough laugh. "That was Hacker's plan," he thought. "Start with a big, obtuse power attack to undertake and take away the ill-equipped, then grow it in successive layers with an ever-increasing number of complex manifestations, until we are invaded. And later, at that exact moment, add a supportive correspondence from an old flame, which we read and then eventually find ourselves beaten. However, an old flame, this is often one Wizard that will not succumb to your stunt. I'll guess that a Troyon is covered up inside that message, and I am getting to find it. You shouldn't have been so sloppy, Hacker. 'Old friend' is correct. You sent me a message from Pass Quay, the Lock maker. However, he's not with us, you fool," he spat as he got a Cleaner from his store of spells and sent it to collect the message.

The Cleaner hurried straight through the mass of cottage and up the edge of the blasting firewall. On getting there, the Cleaner opened an entrance to permit the suspicious correspondence through. No sooner had the message come inside when the Cleaner scooped it up and quarantined it in a different smaller firewall. No matter how enthusiastically the letter attempted to get away, it was caught quickly by the cleaner, who, with all the delicacy of a student specialist, continued to destroy the message until it found the Troyon, alongside an Executor spell, shrouded somewhere inside. The Troyon and the Executor withdrew as far in the terminated statement as they might, then clustered together for comfort and murmuring like cornered cats because the Cleaner drew closer. At long last, they finished the frightful examination. The filter constrained what survived from them through the smaller firewall, leaving a heap of singed ashes on the bottom, and then came back to the cottage, where it dumped its discoveries into the cauldron for further assessment.

The Wizard was pleased that they had taken care of the immediate risk. However, he checked again on the rest of the wizarding network and was surprised at what he found. There, right ahead of him, the cauldron had changed color once again, this time adopting a red tone, with angry yellow images floating on its surface. As he considered the characters, his face withered, and he began trembling with fierceness and sadness. "Hacker, you are malevolent, sly dog," he mumbled between gritted teeth. "So that was your real plan, eh? Delay until I'd caught your suspicious note, then use the gateway that my Cleaner opened to face me? Threads? I despise threads!" And indeed, outside the cottage, over a thousand Threads had started opening up in the firewall, changing it from a considerable obstruction of fireside into some extravagant Swiss cheddar. They were tiny and harmless-looking things, but lengths of white cotton in appearance; however, they might be relentless once they entered the firewall. Suddenly, it occurred to The Wizard what Hacker truly needed. Indeed, control of the magical web and the capacity to destroy the domain was his actual plan. However, to try to do this, he was going to attempt to catch the Kernel.

The Wizard looked behind him into the furthest corner of the cottage. There, suspended between two woven pecan shafts, overcoming any barrier on the ground and roof, was the Kernel: the soul and heart of every sorcerer's being. Usually, it just sparkled a black and green color because it consistently pushed through various spells, collecting the resultant magical vitality later. However, the fight continued outside, it flared and twirled even more splendidly and alarmingly than the cauldron had done. This made it a clear objective for the infringing threads. Once they received it, they might produce such vast numbers of lines that the Kernel would be covered and rendered useless to any who tried to use it.

Understanding that he had only seconds to act, the Wizard rotated to his wooden glyphs and made the one potion that he knew would render all portals closed. With a groan of alleviation, he watched the cauldron one after the other. Closing each entrance that opened in the firewall, he halted the destructive attack of the Threads in their stead. Completely different from the remainder of his kindred warriors, the Wizard immediately reestablished his firewall charms and commenced cautiously re-opening portals, each, in turn, waiting with bated breath for the attack to continue. However, no further challenge came. Outside the furious inferno, the remainder of the Bots, Crawlers, Spoolers, Worms, and the feared Threads, yelled and groaned in mounting wrath, all trying to find a route past the hindrance but discovering nonhospitable them. At long last, he finished the work, and with a faucet of his wand, the Wizard counselled the network's guide again. It didn't take too long to understand that Hacker's attack had made a big hit on the magical web. The spots that were most blatant to him were similar red shades as Malvern and Pokier's. The Wizard had presumed that more, which he was unable to see, were the same. With no time to lose, he closed his eyes and re-joined the network, drawing back a little at the absence of sorcerers that showed up before him. Disregarding all ordinary wizard conventions, he simply spoke his discoveries over the network, directing the remainder of the Wizards, Witches, and Sorcerers to perform an 'all portals closed' spell and open them only to people who were vital for them to talk to.

An hour later and with the sun just beginning to poke its head over the horizon, the Wizard began accepting reports from grateful magicians round the land and world that the request had been a triumph which Hacker's fierce hostility had repulsed. With a deep groan of appreciation to the individuals who watch magical society, the Wizard permitted himself to face entirely still. He then strolled over the now quiet cottage to his captivated cooling box, where he pulled back a cut of cold bread, alongside spaghetti sauce, cheddar and a hot dog, and a jug of refreshing water. It had, without a doubt, been a fantastic night, he thought, as he gulped the water down his parched throat and started eating. Also, one that had seen quite a few of his friends wiped from the land. But they had justified it despite all the difficulty, he thought.

For now, every magical creature in the domain under his protection, including Fairies, Goblins, even the tiny Darkling's, were safe and living in bliss. As the Wizard filled his stomach with food and drink, he closed his eyes and set his mind on the next task. The mantra: "My Chi is more grounded than your Chi," quietly reverberating around his head and moving oddly away and rebounding from the walls of the cottage as well.

Outside, the sun was high in the sky, and the day was assuming the dim sheen of mid-summer. All around the cottage, harmony ruled. The cabin looked only like another country home to a passer-by, settled in a bit of clearing in the encircling woodland. Now, just for a second, a fox running past the cottage door was transformed into something colossal and fierce, without even seeing it in the least. Now, that's the type of cottage that it might be best to simply avoid.

Betty The Secret Princess

Long ago, there was a gorgeous girl named Betty. She lived with her family in a simple home in an ordinary neighborhood.

Although her family loved her without a doubt, she felt that her Mother, Father, and Sister were all particularly plain.

Betty wanted to move and longed to one day become an acclaimed artist, and she also liked to sing and hoped to become a well-known vocalist. But meanwhile, Betty had a mysterious life, a life not even her Sister, Mother or Father knew about.

Betty was eagerly deciding how to become a Princess!

Nobody in the whole world knew about this, except for one person. His name was Edward, and he was secretly becoming a Prince.

He and Betty were old friends and would go on long walks together. Edward would tell Betty how to turn into a Princess. "Why, my future Princess," he would say, "You should look with your Princess eyes, and then, you'll see the gorgeous Pixies sparkling among the trees."

Sure enough, when Betty looked through her future Princess eyes, she could see the gorgeous sparkling Fairies, just as Edward had said.

One day they went for a walk on the edges of the dark forest. Edward suddenly shouted to Betty, "Look, my future Princess, there's a pure white Unicorn hiding away in the dark forest!" And indeed, when Betty looked deeply into the forest together with her new future Princess's eyes, she could see the gorgeous, innocent Unicorn hiding behind the trees.

Betty returned home that night and was so delighted that she didn't even know what was on her plate for supper. Still eating a reasonably large slice of her Mother's meatloaf (which she secretly hated), she also ate three little bits of broccoli without one grumble.

Her Mother was so happy that she gave her an enormous pudding bowl for dessert, with extra topping on top.

Her Sister wasn't very proud of this new development and whined until she, as well, was given a small bowl of pudding with whipped cream on top. A moment later, she sent the two girls upstairs to finish their homework, which neither of them was excited about.

The next day, Edward and Betty happily took their regular walk when Betty thought she heard a voice calling up from a steel sewer grate in the ground.

She visited the grate and called down, "Is there anybody down there?" Edward ran over as well, and the two of them heard a fragile ladylike voice call back. "Oh, please help me! I'm a Queen and I am stuck down here in this unpleasant sewer, and there's a fierce Dragon after me!"

Betty looked boldly at Edward and said, "We should save her, my Prince; it's our obligation as a future Princess and Prince to assist those in trouble!" Edward groaned and waved, "I guess you're right, Betty. Something must be done quickly."

Edward was becoming somewhat disgusted with this game, and all he really wanted to do was take a nice long nap. But he knew Betty wouldn't yield, so he grabbed her hand and yelled, "Okay, now!" and they pulled hard on the grate to open it, and down they went, into the dark, terrifying sewer.

Betty and Edward both landed on their feet, but they were immediately confronted with a fierce, fire-breathing angry Dragon. He was perplexed to see that somebody intruded on his future supper and straight away started fighting them. He snarled so noisily that splendid eruptions of orange flares blew out of his two green nostrils, but Betty wasn't scared.

"Please, Prince, we need to guard the Queen!" she cried and grasped his hand into hers. It had been not a second too early because the fierce Dragon was currently moving toward the Queen and licking his devilish, green Dragon lips, expecting a tasty royal supper. They could see that she was a true Queen. She was lovely and never cried once. She demonstrated no fear but told them that she had been kidnapped and barbarously tossed into the sewer by an evil witch.

Just in time, the darkness crammed with light as many beautiful winged Pixies of all shapes and sizes slid down into the blackness and emitted their beautiful colors of splendid shading in a rainbow of red, blue, green, orange, yellow, purple, and pink. So much light filled the sewer that the Dragon got confused and fled to hide.

Without a moment's delay, Edward picked up the Queen and took Betty's hand, and together they left the sewer and went back into the luxurious daylight. Edward tenderly laid the Queen down on the grass and murmured, "Well, thank heavens for the Pixies."

He was exhausted. This wasn't quite what he had anticipated. But Betty's eyes were sparkling, and she delicately smoothed the Queen's brow to comfort her.

The Queen's eyes fluttered and opened. Slowly she sat up. Delicately she said to Edward and Betty: "Only a real Prince and Princess could have saved me." The Queen told them: "Betty, you'll become Princess Betty and rule my castle reasonably and evenhandedly. Edward, you'll be knighted and from this point forward are going to be referred to as Sir Edward. Once I get older and am not the Queen, you two will take over from me and rule the entire kingdom."

Princess Betty smiled and sparkled in the early evening's brilliant light until she noticed that she could see the Fairies twinkling in the dark starlight and watched as the beautiful Unicorn trotted along through the trees.

Even though Edward was delighted to be promoted to Prince, he wanted to take a nap. Therefore the Queen laid her hand upon Edward, and he happily sat down in the grass for a long-awaited extended rest. Meanwhile, Betty walked around with the Queen in the beautiful dusk, a real Princess finally.

Lottie And The Fabulous Whale

It was a gorgeous bright day. Lottie and her dog Max sat in their seashore cottage. As they sat, Lottie's mind wandered as she looked out into the vast ocean. Then out into the sea, she saw the big fin of a giant Whale. Suddenly, it blew a spout from its blowhole. To her pleasure, she immediately noticed that it had not been water; instead it had been glitter! It was a magic Whale in the world. Lottie ran to the seashore as quickly as her flip-flops would carry her! She called out the Whale by his name since she knew him well.

"Fabulous Whale," she shouted! "Fabulous Whale, please come here." To Lottie's pleasure, he turned and, with a spout of glitter, swam over to her.

The Fabulous Whale swam straight up to the seashore, getting as close as he could to little Lottie. His vast head shifted from side to side as he tried to look at her with both eyes. Eventually, he settled to look with one eye.

"Hi, Fabulous Whale," she said.

"Hellloooooo Looottie," roared the incredible animal. "How is my little friend today?"

"Not good, sadly, Whale."

"Awwww, poor Lottie," the Whale warbled. He let out a deep groan that reverberated through the seashore. She stood on an enormous purring cat. (To get closer to the whale?)

"Would you be able to turn me into a Whale?" she asked sadly.

"Well, there's one exceptionally extraordinary thing I can do." He turned and swam back into the sea. Lottie watched, interested, as he swam away. As she started to think he was leaving her, he turned back around. As he came, he got faster and closer. He continued to swim faster and faster, staying on the brink of the shore. More quickly, he swam until suddenly he turned straight up and leapt into the air! He turned his massive body inconceivably effortlessly then slammed back into the water!

A rush of water splashed far away from him, slamming over the seashore and Lottie.

When she had wiped her face clear of seawater, Lottie looked up just in time to see the Whale leaving. He called back, "Goodbye, Lottie. I hope this works." She shook as a cold shiver ran directly through her entire body. Lottie giggled and was pleased to have talked to her friend. But she wondered when the enchantment would work and hoped she wouldn't feel sick.

The Whale swam away, satisfied with himself. He knew that he was pretty fabulous but not enchanted. The Whale could not repair Lottie. That shiver wasn't magic; it had been seawater soaking into her jeans. But he could make his friend feel better, which was all that mattered.

The Wizard That Overlooked

Many years ago, there was a sympathetic wizard named Accabus. Most wizards and witches live secretly, in disconnected places from mortal creatures. Yet, Accabus preferred humans and went round the world from town to town, helping them whenever he could.

His robes, which had once been a deep, rich purple bound with gold, were now torn and worn, a bit like his Wizard's hat. However, his long white beard, which flowed down his stomach, was as grand as can be.

One late winter, he happened upon another town that he hadn't seen before.

He realized something wasn't right when he saw the blue auras of the townspeople. They looked frightened of him until they understood who he was. The people knew all about his benevolence.

The field surrounding the town lacked the wheat and vegetables that the majority of locals grew to take care of themselves. Accabus stood on the sector's peak and looked as hares, hedgehogs, and even dogs walked around it, not even once stepping on the dirt.

Accabus visited a Farmer and stated, "Your field is in poor condition."

"We do not have any idea why but since we settled here, we haven't been able to grow one thing." The Farmer clarified.

Accabus tapped the Farmer on the shoulder and told him not to worry.

"Stay back," he instructed.

Lifting his wooden staff high, Accabus yelled, "Terrible spirits of hatred not invited by man, leave this land and return to where you came from!"

He then struck the bottom hard three times. The bottom began to shake, and a wave shot out over the sector. Out of nowhere, a hare ran from behind a tree into a gap in the field. It was followed by a dog chasing a cat.

"I bet you'll be able to plant your crops now," Accabus said with much amusement.

Whenever he went through that way, corn and potatoes were now growing in the fertile soil.

As the years passed, gossip spread from town to town that something wasn't right with Accabus. Not many saw him, and the people that did see him said he wasn't benevolent and accommodating anymore; in fact, he looked dismal and desolate.

One day, a little Boy saw him sitting by the side of the road with his head in his hands, crying. "Are you okay, sir?" he inquired.

Accabus didn't reply.

"If not," the Child said brazenly, "go into the Forest of Sorrow." He then ran off, chuckling.

Many people considered the Forest of Sorrow, and Accabus concluded that he should probably check it out because sadness was all he felt now. Wizards can help fix others, yet they cannot repair themselves.

Once every month, when the moon is full, the forest beams with glaring radiance. Light pink berries show abreast of the topmost branches of the trees. A sweet fragrance comes from the berries, which, when inhaled, cures a troubled heart.

Accabus didn't know that you should never spend an hour in the forest when the moon is full. He had been travelling the whole day and was exhausted. When he reached the middle of the forest, he sat at the bottom of a tree and fell sound asleep.

He wandered out of the forest the next day, feeling happy and free.

Whatever his worry had been, it had left, but unfortunately so had his memory.

Before long, it became clear that he also didn't realize that he was a wizard aside from not knowing his name. He could not help people because he did not know any spells or how to use his wooden staff.

Going by the happy yet devoid look everywhere on his face, an older Woman knew that he had been to the Forest of Sorrow and stayed too long; she had seen that look before.

She told Accabus that if he wanted to recollect who he was and recover his powers, he would need to seek out the Yellow Spotted Mungus bug and eat its heart. "You can find them in the forested area on the brink of Hollow Point, but be watchful because they have an extended sharp stinger that's said to be poisonous."

The Wizard didn't even know that he needed to recover his memory because he felt proud of how he was.

But alas, it was concern for the little Girl that redefined his perspectives.

The little Girl searched him with pleading eyes that were continually running, like her nose. She had what everybody had thought was a cold; however, it never went away.

She had been like this for half a year now.

"Do not worry, my child," Accabus said, patting the Girl's head. "I will come back after a few days, and I will help you." Accabus entered the forested area, but it took him two days to seek out the rare Yellow Spotted Mungus bugs.

He grasped one tenderly, but it was such a gorgeous animal that he realized he was unable to do it. "Try not to worry, my little friend," he told the bug, "I'm not going to hurt you." The bug suddenly sunk his stinger into the Wizard's hand.

"Hello," Accabus said in shock. "I told you I would not hurt you."

"It is because you plan no mischief that I have given you what you search for," the bug replied. "The fix is in our venom, so there's no reason to kill us and eat our hearts."

The Wizard began to feel unsteady as his memories began to flood back. "Thank you, is there anything I can do for you now?" he asked the bug.

"Maybe you'll get the message out among different witches and wizards to quit hunting us for his or her potions," the bug answered sadly. "There aren't many of us folks left, you know, but I will do what I can," Accabus guaranteed.

He went back to the town where the Girl with the ceaseless cold lived. She ran up to him with trust in her eyes. He delicately set his hand on her head and stated, "Cold in this child, get away and find another to torment." Her eyes and nose stopped running, and she greeted him with the best smile he had ever seen.

The wizard Accabus could not recall why he had gone into the Forest of Sorrow, but alas, the forest was no more. All the years of trouble and distress it had caused were finally over.

The other witches and wizards could not acknowledge his pleas to let the Yellow Spotted Mungus bug be as they also vanished like the forest. However, the legend of Accabus, the benevolent Wizard, lives on.

The Teddy Bear

A cushioned Teddy Bear once lived inside a chest box in a small boy's room. The Boy would open the toy chest every day and get the fragile Teddy Bear out to play to the Bear's delight.

As the Boy grew up, newer and more splendid toys came into the toy chest. Most of them could perform special tricks. Some moved a distance when the Boy pressed a button; others jumped. But the Teddy Bear had no special tricks. It wasn't a big surprise that the Boy began to select the more splendid new toys as time flew by, and the delicate Teddy Bear became lonely.

When night came, and all the toys are back inside the toy chest, the more splendid toys would talk proudly about the exciting things they might do. The Teddy Bear was always quiet. He had nothing to talk about.

There was one other toy in the toy chest that looked like the Teddy Bear. Cowboy Horse was also a fragile and cushioned toy, but he was old. A notable portion of his hair was gone, and he had only one eye left. Cowboy Horse said to Teddy, "Fragile toys like us are the fortunate ones. We get loved the most, and the more we keep getting the love, the more real we become!"

"What is real?" the Teddy Bear asked.

"Being real is the best," Cowboy Horse said. "You can move when you want to move. When you are real, if you're loved, you can express your love back."

This news was exciting to the Teddy Bear. But how could that ever happen as long as he was stuck in the toy box? The Boy was only playing with toys that would do remarkable things.

One chilly evening, Nana, the babysitter, opened the duvet of the toy chest. She said in a bustling tone, "Goodness, dear! That walking doggie is gone. I should find something different for the boy!" Nana chose the Teddy Bear amongst the toys in the toy chest and gave it to the Boy shortly after.

This started another happy time for the Teddy Bear that would now get all the attention he craved from the Boy. At nighttime, the Boy would hold the Teddy Bear in a tight embrace. In the morning, the Boy would teach the Teddy Bear how to make little gaps under the sheets. If the Boy went outside the house or as far as the park to play, he would take the teddy bear along.

Soon, lots of the Teddy Bear's fur became matted down with all of the cuddling and holding. Its pink nose became less pink with all the Boy's kisses. But the Teddy Bear couldn't have cared less. He was where he wanted to be. He was happy.

One day, the Boy got sick. His forehead burned from a fever. The Doctor had travelled from a remote town to see the Boy. Nana walked back and forth in the hallway in fear for the Boy's life. Day after day, the Boy stayed in bed with the Teddy Bear beside him. There was nothing the Teddy Bear could do to help him get better but to remain in bed, as well, without fail.

When finally, the Boy showed signs of improvement, there was a great relief around the house – everyone rejoiced. Before the Doctor left, he said that the Boy must go to the beach and play there. "How great!" thought the Teddy Bear. The Boy had talked happily about the beach and its white sands and vast blue sea on many occasions.

"Shouldn't something be done about this old Bear?" Nana asked the Doctor.

"That old thing?" asked the Doctor. "It's brimming with scarlatina germs. Burn it without a moment's delay and get him another bear!"

So the gardener tossed the Teddy Bear into a sack alongside the Boy's bedsheets and old clothes and tons of garbage. Nana had told the gardener to take the old stuff to the backyard and burn them.

The Gardener was overly occupied with picking the beans and peas before dusk, so he abandoned the sack. "I will do it tomorrow," he said. The bag wasn't tightly knotted, and the Teddy Bear fell out. The next day when the Gardener got the bag to burn it, Teddy wasn't in it.

The Teddy Bear had gotten far away from the Boy and the house when it began to rain. As he got wetter and wetter from the heavy downpour, he reminisced over his good memories with the Boy, and it dawned on him that he will never feel love from him again. The Teddy Bear was sad. A teardrop fell down his cheek and hit the grass under his feet.

Suddenly, at exactly where the tear fell, a flower grew up. Then, the bud of the flower opened. A little Fairy appeared! "Little Bear," said the Fairy. "Do you recognize who I am?" "I wish I did," said the Teddy Bear.

"I am the Fairy that takes care of toys that are well loved," said the Fairy.

By then, the Teddy Bear was pitiful and had lost all of his fur. The pink coating in his ears had quite a while ago turned dark. His brown hair, once new and splendid, was now nearly black.

"The time has come for me to make you real," said the Fairy.

"I think I remember the word real," said the Teddy Bear. "Now, what was it Cowboy Horse had said? Oh yes, once you are real, you'll move when you want to move. If you're loved, you'll love back." He thought to himself.

With one little wave of the Fairy's wand, teddy felt different. Tickly. Out of nowhere, his two legs could move! A fly perched on Teddy Bear's head, and it was being annoying; quickly, the hand nearest shot up to the Teddy Bear's head to scratch it off.

"So this is real!" said Teddy Bear. "I can move when I want to move!"

"I will show you some new friends," said the Fairy. Then, the Fairy took the Teddy Bear to a group of other Bears who loped and played about. They were all incredible friends.

Time had gone by, and the Boy has now fully recovered.

A moment later, the Boy visited the backyard to play. A few bears jumped out from the trees. One Bear was all black, another was all white, and the other was brown all over. That one stepped the closest to the Boy.

The Boy thought, "Hmm, this Bear looks a lot like my old Bear that was lost when I got sick. Oh, I loved that Bear!" The Boy didn't realize that he was standing in the presence of his favorite toy and that his affectionate love was the reason behind the Teddy Bear becoming real.

A Penguin, A Dark Egg, And An Island

At sunrise, I heard a thump; it had been Salon. He told me that the Dark Wizard had caught Princess Latin. He gave me a survival kit and a map.

"I will provide you with an admonition; I cannot guarantee that once you take a pill, it'll provide a specific outcome," Salon said. I gathered the survival kit, the map, and my trusty sword and hurried to my little wooden raft. It had been a chilly and harsh journey to the ice sheet.

Finally, I made my way to the igloo where my trusty penguin companion Leo was.

"What!" I exclaimed. My penguin companion now had one arm and one eye. "What happened to you?" I ask him. He reveals to me that he was chasing fish for his dinner, and all of a sudden, a dangerous great white shark ate his entire arm and right eye.

"Come with me, I will get you another arm and face," I told him. So we started the long journey to the closest blacksmith and gave Leo the penguin another face and arm. He also gives some very surprising ice pillar controls to freeze enemies together with his new arm. So we began our journey and sailed to a close-by island to rest. We stopped our ship and walked through the serene town to the dark caverns. Fortunately, I installed a stunning glimmer of sunshine into Leo's new mechanical eye. We walked through the cavern until we saw an unwelcome shadow before us. We stopped quickly. The shadow was still distant.

"Be careful," I tell Leo, "The shadow creep could see us." We came to a stop; there were two passages, "Which one should we try?" Leo asks.

"I think we should first check whether there's a secret button around here because there's tons of room between the two passages," I reply.

"Good idea," says Leo, so we search and search, and afterwards, finally, Leo found one and pushed it. A tiny entryway opened between the two passages. We walked through. There were a few bugs and bats, but I dealt with them. Leo is frightened of spiders and bats, so he stayed behind me. We finally found some light, and then we were back outside. I could see a dark low cloud out at sea; the dark wizard was planning some mischief. We sailed to the mansion island, but a giant Dragon was guarding it, so we decided to reroute and visit another close-by island with a blacksmith shed. I found a silver sword and plunged it into a pool of molten silver, then I pounded it into shape and made it extremely sharp. Then, Leo found a tiny island that was shining with gold. Leo cooled my sword, and afterwards, we set sail to the shining gold island. Once we arrived, we saw that it had a lake of molten gold. Once we got out of the boat, Leo came across a vine, and an old locked ground entryway opened. I saw many different suits. I put a navy and white suit on with wall climbing gloves, and Leo got a ninja suit with a jetpack. We also got some potent weapons. We flew back to the Dragon's château, fought the monster, and flew to the gliding island that had the Dragon's palace with Princess Latin trapped inside.

Leo gave me a quick pill, and afterwards, the Nadia spring boots from the survival kit. I took the speed pill and wore the spring boots, and immediately, like a comet, I shot through the air and put my blazing sword into the rear of the terrible Dragon. But the Dragon didn't die from such a powerful attack. I tell Leo to use his ice shaft to freeze the dragon's wings. Finally, the Dragon collided with the ocean. I quickly pulled my sword out of the Dragon and returned to land safely. Then I saw an unusual animal in the distance continuously drawing closer. It seemed as if it had some pointy jewel with it. The Dragon awoke. I wondered where the Princess and the Evil Wizard were and when he would retaliate for revenge.

The Dragon jumped out of the ocean and crashed onto the island next to me. Leo shoots huge ice pieces at the Dragon, but it was futile. I nudged Leo to frost my sword and that I'll spring over the island and cut the Dragon's legs off. Then, I saw a trap on its tail with Princess Latin inside. I hit the Dragon once more in the ribs and raced to grab Princess Latin. I cut the mine (trap?) off the tip of the tail and set Princess Latin free.

"Are you alright?" I ask.

"Yes," she replies.

"Where is that the Evil Wizard?" I continue, "I haven't any idea," she answers.

"Leo, you watch Princess Latin. I'm going to look for the Evil Wizard." I bring my sword and head to the ship and sail to the dead mountains. I knew I was close to the location when I saw an old mansion on the very best point of the most important mountain.

I could tell the Evil Wizard was there.

I parked my ship and commenced my journey up the dead mountains. I need to reach the most peaceful place by continuing the long journey up the mountain.

First, I struggled with people-eating spike plants. Then I fought tiny mushrooms with harmful worm lances. Lastly I fought evil dwarves with magical freezing powers.

Finally, I reached the Evil Wizard's dark den. I kicked open the old wooden door, pulled out my mighty sword, and slowly snuck in. I was sneaking in when I saw two speeding walls close to try and smash me; I used my penguin-like reflexes and got out of there in time. I ran up the old cobblestone steps and saw a shadow at the opened doorway. I bounced in and sank my sword into the Evil Wizard. It got him in the stomach, right where I pointed it. I ran up to him with my sword out, so he was unable to get away. He was dead, and it broke all his spells. The Princess was safe, all because of me, Knight Medin, the relentless.

The Magical Unicorn

A long time ago, a unicorn named Shine lived in the enchanted woods where fairies and mythical creatures also resided. There was something special about this place. You couldn't get there by walking or in a car. You could only get there by falling asleep and dreaming of it.

Shine's owner was a fairy, and her name was Princess Annie. Annie lived in a substantial sparkly palace, and pearls encompassed the beautiful stable where Shine lived.

There were tons of other unicorns with gleaming manes and tails. But Shine was the sole unicorn who did not shimmer like the others, which caused her to feel sad and desire action.

Annie always refused to allow her housekeepers to clean Shine's stable. She did it all herself without the assistance of others. One morning, Annie visited Shine's stable to clean it as she always does, but Shine wasn't there. "Shine has run away!" Annie said. She was so distraught that she decided to hop onto another unicorn, ride into the enchanted woods, and look for Shine.

Meanwhile, Shine was wandering through the enchanted woods when she saw a gorgeous shimmering tree. The tree had a symbol on its wide trunk that said, 'You may have one wish.'

When Shine was close to making a wish, Annie and the other unicorn showed up; Annie returned Shine to the palace, and for the remainder of that day, Shine was brooding about the magical tree and, therefore, the wish she wanted to come true.

The next day Shine decided to go away from the palace stables and revisit the magical tree. She finally got an opportunity and made her way to the tree. When she got there, she wished to possess wings and shimmer like other unicorns. A whirlwind blew, and eventually, Shine had beautiful pink and purple sparkly wings, and she gleamed with shimmering gold. She had never felt such happiness before.

She ran as quickly as possible back to the palace, where the other unicorns praised her beautiful gold and pink and purple wings.

Shine was never troubled again and lived happily ever after in the enchanted woods with Princess Annie and every one of her beautiful unicorns.

The Valiant Princess

In the kingdom of Helena lived a lovely Princess called Nova. Queen Liana would put in great effort to see the Princess behave like a proper lady but to no avail. Princess Nova is a free-spirited girl who prefers to train with a sword and get dirty. One day, Nova is riding her horse when she sees a handsome young man working in the fields near the countryside. She was intrigued by him and decided to speak to him. He tells her that his name is Jack and he's a farmer employed by Chester Northfield. They talk for a really long time about how different their lives are. She spoke of her life as a Princess, and he about his life as a farmer. He tells her that he doesn't enjoy farm work and appreciates the finer things in life, more like reading books and writing poetry. After talking for a while, Nova decides to assist him with his work, and she loses track of her time. Suddenly she realizes that she is late for her Princess training and leaves very abruptly.

When Nova gets back to the castle, she walks into the royal hall where her mother is waiting. She is covered in dirt, and her hair is a mess. When Queen Liana sees Nova and realizes that she has destroyed her dress, she is furious and sends Nova to her room to wash and read books like a real Princess.

Heartbroken that she didn't even get the chance to inform her mother about the marvelous young man she met, Nova storms up to her room and shuts the door behind her. She doesn't leave until supper time, and even when she does come down for dinner, she refuses to talk to her mother.

Later that night, after everyone in the castle had gone to bed. Nova sneaks out of her room and through the excellent hall, and out of the court. She reached for her sword and raced off on her horse into the forest. She wanted to be alone with her thoughts.

On her way, she passes the area where she meets Jack and sees the light on in one of the stables. Curiously, she takes her horse over to the stables. When she peeks through a window, she sees Jack lecturing one of the horses. He was reciting some poetry. While it had been beautiful poetry, Nova was confused, it was past midnight now, and Jack should be in bed, or at least at home.

She ties her horse up outside and slowly enters the stables. Jack sees her and looks happy but also scared. He keeps telling Nova that she can't be there, that it's too dangerous. Confused, she tells him that she knows how to handle horses, and she doesn't think that they're dangerous in the least. Finally, Jack sighs and tells her that he hasn't been candid with her. He confirmed that he worked for Chester Northfield, and that he liked reading books and writing poetry, but he wasn't actually a farmer. He was an assassin hired by Chester to kill King Lukas, Nova's father. Shocked and hurt, Nova pulls out her sword and challenges him to a duel, which Jack declines. He tells her that he's changed since she had spoken to him; he doesn't now think that all royalty are arrogant and mean. He tells her that he is not going to go through with the work, and he would be turning himself in, in the morning. Nova lowered her sword as he continued to mention that he was only in the stables so he could say goodbye to his favorite horse, a gorgeous black stallion named Jeb. He told Nova that, although he was not afraid of going to jail, he was worried about Jeb because he was the only one taking care of him. Chester never fed him, and he never cared for him because he didn't like Jeb.

After hearing all of this, Nova is still infuriated but understanding. She tells Jack that she doesn't blame him and she would forgive him entirely if he helped her catch Chester and turn him in. He agrees and plans to lock him in his house while he's asleep and wait for Nova to get her knights to arrest him.

When Nova returns with the knights, they go to arrest Chester. They find plans to kill King Lukas and the other royal household members hidden inside a locked safe. When Nova returns to the castle with Chester and Jack, her mother was initially distraught, but also very happy because she just wanted Nova to be happy and alive. Nova and Jack tell Queen Liana the entire story and how Jack was willing to turn to servitude as punishment for being an assassin. Queen Liana instead decides that he should be Princess Nova's royal assistant since they work so well together. She then tells Nova that she's pleased with her and needs her to be the knight supervisor, which means she does not have to continue her princess training. Shocked, Nova asks her mother why she has had such a sudden change of heart. She tells Nova that if it weren't for her out keeping watch alongside the knights, the King would have been murdered. The Queen realized that it would be for the good and safety of the entire kingdom to permit the Princess to command the knights and guard the realm.

So they lived their lives happily ever after, with Princess Nova leading the knights and Jack as her right-hand man.

The Princess And The Dragon

Long ago in Spain, there was a kingdom needing a Princess. The dominion sat at the mountain's foot. The name of the hill was La Montana. The King and Queen there had been trying to possess a toddler for several years. All their counselors had offered them a lot of guidance.

"Your majesties," the Duke stated, "if you distribute desserts around nighttime, this may be a sign to the storks that you simply need an infant. The stork will then go up to the mountain and present to you an infant." The King commanded the Royal Confectioner to make up his very best jams and desserts. They put a bushel of desserts at each passage to the palace. The subsequent morning the King and Queen ran from crate to crate, checking for their child. However, all they found were many desserts.

"Your majesties," the Marquis stated, "request that the Royal Physician makes a pill that the queen will take to become pregnant." Therefore the King commanded the Royal Physician to make a pill for the Queen. The doctor went white and shook from his cap to his boots. He did not have any idea of what to put into a pill to make a child! Instead, he discreetly descended to the kitchen and took one of the jams. He offered this to the Queen at bedtime, together with her cup of hot cocoa. The Queen could hardly rest. But when she awakened the following morning, there wasn't an infant insight.

"Your majesty," the Countess stated, "request that the Royal Baker bake you a toddler." The King commanded the Royal Baker, but the Queen shut that down immediately. Baking a toddler didn't seem right.

"It's sad," the poor Queen cried. The Queen resigned to her garden, where she sat under the purple shade of a jacaranda tree and sobbed. She so wanted to have a toddler, but she didn't imagine she could ever have one. As she sat down crying, the old Gardener happened to hear her and wandered over.

"Your highness, for what reason does one cry?" he inquired.

"The kingdom needs a princess, and for that I need a baby. We've made many attempts, but I do not think it'll ever happen," answered the Queen tragically. The gardener, who adored the Queen like a father who cherishes his daughter, couldn't stand to see her crying.

"There is an old legend," he started, "that my wonderful granddad told me about before he passed on. It's a mystery and cannot be imparted to anybody just in case they exploit the enchantment." "Enchantment?" the Queen asked through her tears.

"Enchantment," the Gardener answered. "A cavern is found high on La Montana, the Cave of Altamira. This cavern is home to a Dragon. It's known that if you're in urgent need, you ought to take treasure up to the cavern, then you ought to draw a picture of the thing you would like the foremost upon the walls of the cavern and sleep beneath your drawing. At the start of the day, if the Dragon acknowledges your gift of fortune, then the thing you would like most is going to be there once you wake. Maybe you could visit the cavern and see if the Dragon will offer you the child you desire."

The Queen expressed gratitude toward the old Gardener and rushed to assemble food and fortune, and saddle her horse. Without even bidding farewell to the King, she rode north as fast as her horse could go. All that day, she scanned through the mountain for the Cave of Altamira. Before sunset, the Queen at long last found the cavern. She slid from the saddle and attached her horse to a close by tree. The Queen gathered the fortune she had brought for the dragon and immediately took it into the cavern. Setting it on the ground, she ventured into her pocket, and out of nowhere, realized that she lacked anything to draw with.

She quickly went back to her horse as the sun ducked below the horizon and looked through her saddle sacks. However, she was unable to find anything to draw with. The only thing she had left in her pack was an apple and a honey sandwich. Urgently, the Queen grabbed the honey sandwich and hurried once again into the cavern. She inserted her finger into her honey sandwich. She scraped as much of the sticky, brilliant goo onto her finger as she could. Using the honey on her finger, the Queen drew a picture of an infant on the caverns mass. Then, just like the last beams of daylight lit the sky, she tossed herself down on the ground and sobbed. The Queen was sure that each of her endeavors had been in vain, meaning she would never get the child that she so urgently wished she had. She eventually drifted off into a troubled rest filled with dreams of a Dragon and a gorgeous child with with dark curly hair on her head.

While the Queen was dreaming, the King was anxious. When she didn't come back from the garden, he went looking for her. When he could not find her, he requested each individual from the royal house to look for her. They looked through the dominion all night. The following day, the King got on his horse on the patio charging his subjects to be brave. He commanded his Dukes, Marquis, and Knights to search the mountain for their Queen.

Suddenly, out of nowhere, he heard a yell from the castle walls.

"Your highness," cried a gatekeeper, "the Queen is coming!" The King jumped from his horse and raced to the door, filled with questions for his Queen, but when he saw her, he stopped running and stood there, paralyzed. The Queen was carrying a child! The meekest child he had ever seen. The Queen slowly walked over to the lord and put the baby in his arms. He looked down at the small bundle, with short black curls of hair on her head and brilliant eyes gazing at him through long eyelashes. His heart softened on the spot, and he was unable even to ask the Queen where the infant had come from; all he could do was stand and appreciate her.

The King requested a feast be readied, and the whole kingdom be told that they now had a Princess. The Queen named her Altamia out of appreciation for the Dragon's cavern that had given her to them. Everybody in the realm called her Princes Mia el Milagro, Princess Mia the Miracle, and she was a gorgeous child. The sole strange thing about her was that she loved honey. She would eat honey on toast for breakfast, she would eat honey with fruit for lunch, and she would eat honey with pasta for supper.

As Mia grew, she began to approach her mother and ask for someone to play with The King welcomed each child in the kingdom to the palace to find a friend for his child. However, whenever a child entered the castle, the King would find a big issue. He denied any of them returning and to play with his girl.

He said "No" to the Nobleman's small girl because the sole thing she liked was to eat desserts and candy. The lord previously thought his Princess ate too much honey and was concerned that this girl would be a terrible influence.

He said "Never" to the Marquis's kid, as there was something unusual about him. He spent the more significant part of his days up in his room, blending synthetics and making unique smelling mixtures. The lord was worried that he might accidentally transform his child into a frog.

He told the Countess to go away when he saw her coming towards the palace with her girl. He never trusted her after the proposal of baking a toddler in the oven.

As the last kid headed out of the castle, Mia headed to the garden and sat under an identical jacaranda tree that her mom had sat under five years ago. She cried quietly until the Queen decided to seek out her.

"Mia," the Queen said, putting her hand on her girl's shoulder, "have I ever told you the story of how you were born?" The Princess shook her head. The Queen told Mia how eager she was to have a toddler and how long the kingdom had waited for a princess. The Queen also told her about the Dragon in the Cave of Altamira.

"Mom, do you think that I could go to the cavern and ask the Dragon for somebody to play with?" Mia asked.

"Why don't we both go and ask the Dragon together," the Queen suggested.

They visited the kitchen for food, then to the treasury for gifts to offer the Dragon. As they were on the way to the stable where the groomsmen were outfitting their horses, the King saw them and shouted over: "My queen and princess, where are you going?" The Queen told the King that they might ask the dragon in the Cave of Altamira for a friend for the Princess.

"Then I'm going with you. I will be able to affirm the friend, or the Dragon can take them back and find someone else." therefore, the King, the Queen, the Princess, and a score of

Knights took to the road within the hour and headed out north to the mountain to seek out the cavern.

When they showed up, the Queen gave the Princess a charcoal stick, but Mia shook her head.

"If the Dragon can truly give me the friend that I would like, I should draw the image in the same way that my image was drawn." Mia pulled a honey container from her pocket and entered the cavern with her mother and father. As she drew, her parents laid the fortune that they had brought down. When she had finished, each of the three sat down and slept. The Princess longed to enjoy herself with her new friend in the gardens, stables and wander around the palace together. The Queen longed for the right friend for the Princess, who would always assist and be faithful to her little girl. The ruler longed for the bravest knight, always prepared to ride to Mia's aid and who would always protect his girl.

As the sun slowly peaked above the horizon on the next morning, Mia awakened with a start. She looked around, hoping to see if her new friend was waiting, but there was nobody. She thought that perhaps her new friend was still on the way, maybe from deeper inside the cavern. So Mia stood and quietly walked to the rear of the cavern. There she saw a passage, completely covered up by stones. She only just got through the opening and advanced down the aisle. It was exceptionally dark in the cave, and even though Mia knew that she should probably turn back around, she spied what resembled light further up the path. She rushed towards the light, which became more apparent and more evident the closer she got to it.

On the cave's furthest side was an oversized heap of fortune, which sparkled and shined in the candlelight. As she stood gazing, Mia saw with a shock that something was staring back at her. Two round and brilliant eyes were watching her.

Mia was about to head for the passage when somebody addressed her.

"Oh, Princess Mia, you're finally here. Step into the candlelight. I am old, and my sight isn't as it used to be, I'm afraid." Mia ventured further into the cavern. She didn't know where the voice was coming from until she saw a couple of jewels and coins tumbling from the heap of fortune. She gazed upward and saw that the very highest point of the pile was moving. Mia looked on, as first one gem-encrusted leg, then another extended. Then she heard what appeared like large wings fluttering, and an incredible black Dragon landed intensely before her.

"Ooohhh," murmured Mia. "You are beautiful."

"Thank you, Princess. Now with regards to your wish, I have not overlooked or denied you. However, I needed you to return and see your new companion for yourself. It had been a difficult endeavor trying to grant your wish and that of your parents. You wanted somebody to play with while your mom wanted a loyal and accommodating friend. In contrast, your dad wanted a fearless friend who could protect you. The way things are, one child couldn't satisfy all of these wishes."

"Does that mean you're giving me a friend to play with?" Mia asked.

"No, child!" laughed the Dragon, "Because human kids need parents to take care of them too. My enchantment is solid, however, not unreasonably solid. Rather, I have concluded that you simply can help me as well. As I referenced, I'm getting old. I will, soon, need another to take my spot. Once you and your friend have grown, she is going to return here to the cavern to take my spot." Mia's eyes grew as wide as supper plates.

"Do you mean that my friend is going to be a...a Dragon?" Mia asked, amazed.

"It will be a baby Dragon; she is going to play, help and protect you. Will you be happy with a Dragon friend?"

"Goodness, yes! Thank you!" Mia cried, clapping. The Dragon wagged his tail, and behind him was a tiny Dragon, about the size of a large dog. The Dragon had beautiful dark shining scales, the shade of honey, and brilliant eyes that seemed to sparkle. Mia knew this was who had been watching her the first time she entered the cave. She opened her hand to the small Dragon that then came over to visit and sniffed it, and then gave it a quick lick. Mia chuckled. "You may take your friend now, Princess. She is going to know when it is the right time for her to return to the cave and take my place." Mia said many thanks to the black Dragon and turned and walked back down the passage.

She discovered her parents and the knights were just awakening. They were terrified when they saw the Dragon, but when Mia told them this was her new friend, they were amazed. Mia clarified that the Dragon was a friend who could play with her as well as be loyal and help her, but who was also fearless and will protect her if necessary.

"Does she have a name?" the Queen asked. Mia considered it for a few moments and afterwards answered, "Her name is Bella, the most beautiful creature I even have ever seen."

The King, the Queen, the Knight's Mia, and Bella all began their trip back to the stronghold. The black Dragon was correct. Bella was the closest friend that Mia could have had.

They played together, and Bella was savagely loyal and fearless. One of their favorite activities was to explore the open country and find jacaranda trees shrouded in blossoms. Mia would stay under the tree, and Bella would hover over it and flutter her excellent honey-shaded wings so hard that everything shook from the branches. Mia would giggle in delight as she spun around in the purple downpour. When the tree was exposed, the ground covered in a soft purple floor cover, the pair would then toss themselves into the blossoms and play around in them, making flower angels.

In the beginning, the King would send his Knights out together with his female child and her friend whenever they explored the open country. But he honestly did not have to, as Bella was the sole protection Mia needed. A number of times, they might find a wildcat, a lynx, or a pack of wolves, but the savage creatures wouldn't approach the Princess with Bella around, and when a gaggle of criminals happened upon them they were sent fleeing as fast as possible, their ears ringing with Bella's thunder and their backsides burning slightly, due to Mia's fire-breathing friend. As the years went on, and both Mia and Bella became more significant, the King gave his Knights different assignments, leaving Mia and Bella to travel, explore and adventure on their lonesome. In the morning, Mia would sit together with her dad and master all she needed to be a ruler. Toward the evening, Mia and

Bella would pass through the sector, exploring and playing. They might take an excursion to the lake, with honey sandwiches always the lunch of choice for both of them. When Bella had first shown up around the castle, different children had been too hesitant even to come close to her. But slowly, the youngsters understood that Bella was friendly and wouldn't hurt them. Eventually, they came individually to acquaint themselves with the Princess and her honey-hued dragon. As the years passed, different children would occasionally join Mia and Bella on their picnics or explore the open country. On her twelfth birthday, the King arranged for Mia an elaborate birthday celebration, and the castle was filled with children, running and laughing and playing.

The Greedy Dog

Once there was a Dog who was too greedy. There were times where he wished he didn't have his greed. Every time, the Dog would say to himself, "I have learned my lesson. Now, I will never be greedy again." But soon, he forgot his promises and was as greedy as he could be.

One afternoon, the Dog was hungry. He chose to go and look for something to eat. Just outside his home, there was a bridge. "I will search for food on the other side of the bridge. The food there's better," he thought to himself.

He walked over the wooden bridge and began sniffing around for food. Suddenly, he spotted a bone lying in the distance. "Oh, I'm in luck. That looks like a tasty bone," he said.

Without wasting any time, the hungry Dog got the bone and was about to eat it when he thought, "Someone might see me here with this bone, and then, I will have to share it with them. So, I had better return home and eat it." While holding the bone in his mouth, he ran toward his home.

While crossing the wooden bridge, the Dog looked down into the stream. There he saw his reflection. "I can see another dog in the water with a bone in its mouth," he thought. Greedy, as he was, he thought, "How nice would it be to have that bone too. Then, I will have two bones." So, the greedy Dog checked out his reflection and snarled. The reflection growled back, too. This made the Dog angry. He looked down at his reflection and barked, "Wooooooooooooooof! Wooooooooooooof!" When he opened his mouth to bark, the bone in his mouth fell off into the stream. The greedy Dog realized that what he saw was his reflection and not another dog.

But it had been too late. He had lost the bone thanks to his greediness. Now he had to go hungry.

The Princess And The Faithful Knight

Long ago, there was a gorgeous Princess. Her magnificence talks about poets who composed tomes filled to the brim with poems and sonnets dedicated to her majesty in the dominion. Artists filled whole displays with artworks and figures, attempting eagerly to capture her beautiful figure. Her brilliance was outperformed distinctly by her intelligence. Her father, the King, had raised her to be a fair and just ruler.

After a while, her only concern was the bliss and wellbeing of her people.

One fateful day, a handsome Prince came to town. He had come to charm the Princess. They spent some hours together. From hours to days and days to weeks, the beautiful princess began to experience passionate feelings for the charming Prince. Their adoration was talked about in the realm.

One day, the charming Prince took the gorgeous Princess to an obscure mountain at the edge of the deep wood. He began to tell her how much he cherished her. He said she would enter the thick fore and pick him the rarest flower on the planet if she adored him: the scarlet rose. The Princess agreed out of pure dedication to the charming Prince. She went into the deep wood, trying to find the scarlet rose. The sun began to set, and exactly when all seemed to be lost, she stumbled upon it. She went to pick the gorgeous rose and pricked her finger on one of its thorns, and the beautiful Princess fell into a deep sleep. The Prince stood over her body and smiled. It had been his plan from the beginning.

He then stole all of the Princess's wealth.

He had a woman expecting him in another kingdom, and he left the gorgeous Princess in the deep wood. The King held search parties, but they couldn't find her. Months went by until, when, while searching, the King stumbled upon a gorgeous lady shrouded in vines. It was his daughter. He attempted to wake her, but try as he might, she wouldn't wake from her deep sleep. The King lamented over his beautiful girl, taken from him in the prime of her life. He called his counsellors to him, who returned the gorgeous princess to the castle. They laid her down in her bed chamber and considered what to try to do. His consultants considered her to be asleep and decided that the rationale was the toxic substance in the scarlet rose. Once they told the King, he implored them to offer her a remedy, but no antidote existed. They tried every mixture in the realm to wake her, but none would wake the gorgeous Princess. The King's counsels came to him and told him that all they could do was hope that the toxic substance would run its course. The King, infuriated, looked to the dominion for a reason for his daughter's sleep. He didn't find anything until he heard a word from another kingdom of a young Prince who's fortune arose apparently out of thin air. This was the charming Prince that had tricked the gorgeous Princess.

The King then announced that, from that day forward, should a person wish for his daughter's hand, then that man must wait in the kingdom for her to wake. Men from all over the planet came to be by the side of the woman of outstanding excellence. The admirers lined the roads of the dominion. Each attempting to demonstrate his value. Years passed by, and the accounts of the Princess' magnificence blurred and eventually became forgotten Gradually, men began to become bored with waiting and accepted that the gorgeous Princess could never wake. Individually they left the dominion. Days became months, and months became years until the roads, once crammed with admirers, now lie empty. All the admirers had left the gorgeous princess.

Aside from one.

A solitary Knight remained to kneel at her bedside. He had not moved from the second he arrived. His armor had become substantial with rust. Time went on until one fateful day when the Princess at long last awoke. When she opened her eyes, only one kneeled before her: the foremost faithful Knight. As he looked into her recently opened eyes, he told her what had unfolded: The toxic substance, the King's pronouncement, and the way he'd waited for her.

But then, the foremost faithful Knight said something that astounded her. He talked about how he had adored her continuously from afar. He said he had become a Knight with the hope of one day serving her in her court. He moved the gorgeous Princess to tears. She brought in her father, who was happy to see his girl awake once more. Out of his bliss, he promised her anything she wanted. She said she wanted just one thing: the faithful Knight to join her in her court, in any case, not as a Knight, but as her Prince.

They were married the next day, and the kingdom cheered. The dominion would forever tell the story of the gorgeous Princess and the most faithful Knight.

Lisa Prepares A Cake

Tonight, we are going to enjoy a stunning story about my good friend Lisa and the fantastic cake she baked with her Dad!

This cake story will be a lot of fun; I know you'll love learning about the way to bake a cake with Lisa.

Before we start this incredible story, though, we need to make sure that you are comfortable and relaxed enough to listen!

Make sure you've done your entire bedtime routine, so you're able to lay completely still and fall asleep after the story.

If you've not already, have a sip of water, say goodnight to your family, and get cosy in your bed.

Then, we will start with a pleasant and straightforward breathing meditation to assist you in calming your body down so that you'll have an excellent sleep tonight.

Are you ready?

Let's begin with short breathing meditation.

I would like you to imagine that you are holding a balloon in front of your face for this meditation.

Can you do this for me?

Great!

Now, let's imagine that you are taking a pleasant, deep, slow breath in through your nose, then you're getting to blow out through your mouth as if you were trying to fill the balloon up with air!

Starting now, inhale nice and slowly through your nose, filling your lungs up with air.

Now, exhale through your mouth as if you're trying to fill a balloon up with air!

Perfect, let's do that again.

Breathe in slowly through your nose, and now exhale through your mouth to refill your balloon.

Breathe in slowly, filling your lungs all the way, then exhale through your mouth, filling the balloon up with air.

Breathe in slowly, and once more, exhale, filling up the balloon.

One more time, inhale slowly through your nose, filling your lungs up with air.

Now, exhale through your mouth, filling your balloon all the up with air!

Perfect!

Now let's imagine that your balloon filled with air floats away into the night sky, leaving you relaxed and prepared to enjoy a captivating story and an honest night's sleep.

Goodbye, balloon!

One day, Lisa's Dad told her that her Mother's birthday was coming up!

Excited, Lisa started planning out what she could do for her Mother's birthday.

Lisa was only eight years old, so it had been not too easy for her to travel to the shop and find a stunning present to celebrate her Mom.

So, she asked her Dad to help her find a gift and assist her in baking a cake for her mom.

Of course, her Dad said yes, and then in the week before her Mother's birthday, Lisa's Dad took her to the mall to choose a gift for her Mother.

While there, Lisa picked out a gorgeous silver necklace that said "Mom" and had a heart shape around it with three rhinestones in the heart.

Lisa brought it home, wrapped it up, and hid it in her closet so that her Mother wouldn't find it before her birthday.

On her Mother's birthday, Lisa and her Dad went to the kitchen to bake a cake.

They started by gathering all of the supplies they needed.

"What do we need first, Dad?" Lisa asked.

"Well, the recipe says that we need flour, sugar, cocoa, bicarbonate of soda, and salt from the cabinet. Are you able to get those for us, kiddo?" Lisa's Dad asked.

"Absolutely!" Lisa said.

Lisa visited the pantry, opened it up, and grabbed the flour from the bottom shelf, then the sugar, bicarbonate of soda, and salt from the second shelf.

Then, she searched and saw that the cocoa was all the way up on the top shelf.

"Can you grab it for me, please, Dad?" Lisa asked.

"Great manners, Lisa, yes I can." Her Dad said, grabbing the cocoa from the highest shelf and putting it on the counter.

"What now, Dad?" Lisa asked.

"Well, next, we need two eggs, buttermilk, butter, and vanilla." Her Dad answered.

"Great! I can do that!" Lisa said, opening the fridge to fetch the eggs, buttermilk, and butter.

"Where's the vanilla kept?" she asked, searching high and low for it.

"Whoops! That's in the cupboard!" her Dad grinned, going back to the pantry to grab the vanilla.

Lisa giggled and grabbed a bowl out of the cabinet.

"Is that everything?" Lisa asked.

"That is!" her Dad smiled.

Lisa went back to the pantry, grabbed the footstool, and placed it by the counter where the blending bowl was resting.

"Are we able to get started?" she asked.

"We are! But first, we need the measuring cups and spoons! And a spatula." Her Dad said, pulling them out of the cabinet.

"Okay, let's get started!" he said.

"First, we need to measure out the flour. Are you able to measure one and three-quarter cups of flour?" asked her Dad, handing her the measuring cups.

"Absolutely!" Lisa said.

She carefully measured out the flour and poured it into the blending bowl.

"Great, now we'd like two cups of sugar. Are you able to put two cups of sugar into the bowl?" Lisa's Dad asked.

"I sure can." Lisa grinned, adding two cups of sugar to the bowl. "Now, we need three-quarters of a cup of chocolate."

"Okay!" Lisa smiled, adding the chocolate to the bowl.

"Can you add one and a half teaspoons of bicarbonate of soda now, Lisa?" her Dad asked, handing her the measuring spoons.

"Of course!" Lisa said, measuring out the bicarbonate of soda and adding it to the bowl.

"Great, now we'd like three-quarters of a teaspoon of salt."
"Got it!" Lisa said, adding the salt.

A little salt spilt over onto the counter.

"Oops!" Lisa said, looking up at her Dad.

"No problem." He smiled, wiping it away with a damp cloth.

"Now what?" Lisa asked.

"Well, it says here that we now need to combine the dry ingredients."

"Okay!" Lisa answered, using the spatula to combine the flour, sugar, chocolate, bicarbonate of soda, and salt.

The mixture darkened as the chocolate blended in with the other dry ingredients and began to look just like the packaged cakes that her Grandma sometimes purchased when she didn't want to make a cake from scratch. "Great, that looks good, Lisa. Now, let's add the wet ingredients together. Let's start with the eggs." Her Dad said, handing her two eggs.

"Can you do it by yourself?" he asked.

"I sure can!" Lisa smiled, carefully cracking the first egg over the side of the blending bowl.

The side split, and Lisa used her fingers to pry the egg open, revealing gooey albumen and yolk inside.

She dumped the egg into the bowl, then placed the eggshell to the side.

She cracked the next egg, again prying the gooey egg open and letting the albumen and yolk slide into the bowl next to the other egg.

This time, she accidentally got some shell into the bowl.

"Oops! How do I get that out?" Lisa asked.

"Check this out," her Dad said, taking half the empty eggshell and scooping the broken piece out of the batter.

"Woah, how did you do that?" Lisa asked, amazed by how easily her Dad pulled the eggshell out.

"Baker's secret." He winked.

"Okay, now let's add the buttermilk. We'd like one and a half cups of it."

Lisa's Dad said, handing her the buttermilk.

Lisa measured out the milk then poured it into the blending bowl, watching the thick white milk mix alongside the eggs on top of the dry ingredients.

"Done," Lisa said, putting the cup down.

"Great, now let's add the butter. We'd like to melt it first, so I will be able to do this." Said her Dad, measuring out half a cup of butter and placing it in a small pot over a medium heat, stirring it regularly to help it melt.

Once he melted the butter, Lisa's Dad added it to the blending bowl.

"Now, the vanilla. This is often the last ingredient!" said her Dad as he gestured towards the vanilla.

"How much?" She asked.

"One tablespoon." He smiled, handing her the measuring spoons once more.

"Excellent." She grinned, pouring a tablespoon of vanilla into the blending bowl.

"That's it! Mix it up!" Lisa's Dad said.

As she started mixing the bowl, her Dad turned on the oven and readied the cake pans.

Meanwhile, Lisa used the spatula to combine the ingredients in the bowl.

At first, it appeared like they weren't coming together that well, but Lisa kept mixing and mixing.

Soon, all of the ingredients were coming together in a soupy wet mixture.

The batter was relatively wet and thick, but it seemed like it might be delicious once she had finished it.

When Lisa was satisfied that she had mixed it all the way through, her Dad gave it one last go to make sure that it was perfect.

Then, they poured the mixture into two separate cake pans, and her Dad put them in the hot oven for her.

Lisa was so excited to make these cakes for her Mother that she stayed in the kitchen the entire time they were baking.

She sat on the ground in front of the oven, waiting for them to rise.

At first, it seemed like nothing was happening as the cakes sat in the oven baking.

Soon, however, the smell of cake began to fill the house, and the cakes slowly began to rise.

Lisa continued sitting there, watching the whole baking process play out before her very eyes as both of the cakes rose and baked all the way through.

When the oven went off, Lisa stood back as her Dad pulled the cakes out of the stove and poked a toothpick into the middle of them to make sure they had baked all the way through.

"Perfection!" he smiled, showing her that the toothpicks were completely clean upon bringing out the cake.

Lisa's Grandmother had taught her that this meant she had fully baked the cakes, but if the toothpick came out dirty with cake batter, they'd need to bake a little longer.

They let the two cakes rest for a couple of minutes before turning them out onto a drying rack and letting them cool even longer.

Then, they put the icing on top of the first cake and stacked the second cake on top of it.

"A double-decker!" Lisa giggled, watching the large, delicious cake that they had made for her Mother.

They iced the remainder of the cake and then covered it in sprinkles and candles for her Mother's birthday.

Then, they waited for her Mother to get home.

When she did, they lit the candles and showed the cake to her Mother, and her Mother smiled and blew all of the candles out.

"You made this for me?" her Mother asked, scooping Lisa up into a hug.

"Yes, Dad, and I did!" she answered.

"Here, we got this for you, too!" Lisa said, handing her Mother the gift they had bought her.

Lisa's Mother opened it and smiled when she saw the necklace.

"It's perfect," she said, hugging Lisa and her Dad very close. "What an ideal birthday." Lisa's Mother sighed.

The three of them ate the cake and enjoyed a night laughing and playing board games together.

When you want to make something in your life, it is often helpful to understand how to put in the work necessary.

It might seem more straightforward to travel the convenient route and let somebody else do all of the work for you. But then, on the other hand, you do not get the unique feeling of knowing that you did the job yourself.

Doing the work for yourself means you get to feel pleased with the work you have done, and you get to share the impressive results with others.

The good feelings you get inside once you accomplish something special are vital, and they can help you feel even better.

When you want something in your life but you're struggling to remain motivated to achieve it, remember these essential affirmations:

"I am capable of everything."

"I am great at making things happen."

"If I want it, I can create it."

"I can always try again."

"I am okay."

"I can always ask for help."

"Trying counts."

"One step at a time."

The Lion And The Camel And The Jackal And The Crow

There once was a Lion living in a beautiful jungle called Madotkata. He was the Jungle King. His court included a Leopard, a Jackal, and a Crow, alongside other wild animals. They frequently went out together in search of food. One day at some point, the Lion saw a Camel as they were roaming in the jungle.

The Camel was alone; he was far away from his home and ate the jungle's green grass. The Camel was an unusual species that had never been seen by the Lion before. He said, "Let's talk to this animal and ask him where he came from." The Camel spoke to the Crow and the Crow told the Lion, "He is named a Camel, and was born here in the village. His meat has a special taste, and we can kill him and eat him for dinner." But the Lion disagreed with the Crow, claiming,

"Because he is in our jungle, he's our friend. We will not kill him. Talk to him and assure him there won't be any harm here and afterward, bring him to me."

They visited the Camel in line with the Lion's orders and told him they had come here to take him to the Lion. No harm will befall him. They gained his trust then took the Camel to the Lion. They all walked up to the Lion, and the Camel bowed. He explained that he got separated from his party on his way to the jungle.

On hearing such news from the Camel, the Lion said to him, "Oh, if you go back to the village, then you'd need to carry men again. You can sleep in my kingdom in the jungle here and may feast on the jungle's green grass with no fear." The Camel didn't hesitate to accept the offer, and since then, all of them have lived happily together.

One day, the Lion got seriously injured from a battle with an insane Elephant and he couldn't walk. So, he couldn't move around to play or look for food. As days went by, the Lion became very weak due to food scarcity and his festering wounds from battle. The other animals were also beginning to starve because they relied on the Lion for their food. In a few days, when the Lion could not bear his hunger, he ordered the Crow, the Jackal, and the Leopard and said to them, "Please go and find some animal that I can kill even in my feeble state. Then, I can provide food for you all and myself." So all the animals went into the jungle searching for food, but they failed and began to return home.

The Jackal had a thought. He told the Crow, "The food is already here, folks, and there is no point in looking in the jungle. The Camel will supply us all with food for an extended time."

Then the Crow answered him, "What you say could also be right, but the Lion pledged his protection to the Camel. He won't renege on his promise."

The Jackal said, "Let me try. I'll convince the Lion to allow us to kill the Camel and eat him."

The Jackal then visited the Lion and said to him, "Oh King King, we searched around the forest but couldn't find any animals for you. All of us folk haven't eaten in days and we could barely walk upright. If this continues for much longer, we'll all die of starvation. But, if you permit us to slaughter the Camel, his flesh will provide several days of food for us all."

The lion objected, shouting at him, "Shame on you! How am I able to murder the Camel when I promised him his protection in my kingdom? I cannot even think that way." But the Jackal added, "Sir since you assured him of his protection, it might be wrong to kill him. But if he offers himself as your food by himself, killing him and eating him wouldn't be wrong." The Jackal kept trying to persuade the Lion, "Sir, it's our duty to serve our King King, and even in his time of need, if we cannot serve his lord, then what good are we for and who can we live for. Please sacrifice one of us for yourself and others, to stop the remaining folks from dying of starvation." The Lion had nothing to say and instead, he responded, "Please do what you think is best for us all."

After this, the Jackal returned to the other animals and said to them, "Our Master is sick and weak. If anything happens to him, we're going to need to defend ourselves. After looking everywhere in the jungle, we've not found any food. The only way our Master can work is by giving ourselves to him to save his soul. Then, most folks will be spared from starving to death."

Then the animals went before the Lion and told him of their plan. They told the Lion that they could not find any animals for his food.

The Crow was the first to ask, "Sir, we couldn't find an honest animal for your food. So, I give you myself to save yourself from hunger, please accept me as your food."

Suddenly the Jackal interrupted the Crow, "You are too small to supply the Master with a meal, dear Crow. Albeit if he agrees to accept your offer, it simply won't be enough. Your loyalty to your lord is already established, there is no need to please him."

Then he turned toward the Lion and said, "Master, accept me as your meal, please. Kill and eat me to save many of you from going hungry. I would be honored if you'd consider my offer, and I'd find a spot in heaven."

The Lion refused his proposal upon hearing it. The other species started proposing themselves the same way, but the Lion turned down all the offers.

The Camel saw all of this, and he said, "All of them discuss giving themselves so wonderfully, but the Master refuses to kill any of them. I'll attempt to impress the Master myself."

Stepping forward, the Camel said to the other creatures, "You volunteered yourselves, but the Master couldn't eat you because you're the same family as the Lion himself. I want to offer myself to my lord.'

The Camel moved toward the Lion and bowed toward him. He said, "Sir, there is no need to kill all of those creatures. Instead, please eat me. I give myself to you to settle my debts.

If you accept my offer, please, I will be able to find my way to heaven."

Shortly after the Camel volunteered himself, the other animals began to perk up. Because the Jackal had already persuaded the Lion, the Lion fiercely attacked the Camel and killed him.

Even the wise say:

'Whenever you're in the company of wicked people, always keep up a guard. Don't be deceived by their sweet words.'

Max Goes For A Walk

Max, the black lab, loved going for walks.

Every day, he would await his owner to return home so that he could go on a walk together with his friend and enjoy the neighborhood.

Every day after his owner John came home from work, they would go on an exquisite walk, and Max would get to visit all of his friends.

He would see the neighborhood cat, Liza, the neighborhood bulldog, Willy, and the neighborhood hare, Hopper. They would always smile and nod at one another as Max proudly walked next to John. Once they got home, John would always give Max a cookie, and Max would then go and sit down to enjoy his treat. One day, Max eagerly waited by the front entrance for his walk with John.

As he waited, he noticed John appeared to be taking longer than usual.

He sat a little bit longer, expecting John to return home.

Max worried that perhaps something bad had happened when it started getting later, and maybe that John wouldn't be coming home.

Afraid of what might have happened, Max ran to the rear door, and went out of the doggy door, and the back gate.

He jumped up at the gate, trying to look over the top to determine if he could see into the driveway where John always parked his car when he got home.

As he was jumping, the gate shook loose and opened.

Max ran out into the driveway to find that there was no car in view.

So, he began a journey to find John.

Max jogged up the road where he and John usually walked.

As he did, he saw their friend Liza curled in some bushes, enjoying a nap.

On this particular day, Max didn't bark to awaken her to say hello but instead let her sleep as he carried on his way, trying to find John.

He kept jogging until he reached the corner where he would usually take a turn with John.

This time, Max decided to take the left turn in hope that he would find John.

While he ran, he saw their bulldog friend, Willy, sitting in the window of his home; his paws still wet from the walk he had just been on together with his owner Macy.

Knowing that Willy had already finished his entire walk made Max even more worried as he realized how much time had now passed. Willy and Max nodded at one another as Max kept jogging down the road.

Willy barked a few times, but nobody noticed that Max was out without John. When he reached the end of the road, Max grew confused.

This wasn't the way he and John typically went, so he wasn't quite as confident with this route. Although he had done it a couple of times, he wasn't as sure on which way to go.

Off in the distance, he thought he saw Hopper, so he started running that way, sure that this must be the right direction to find John.

Max jogged down a couple of streets, then stopped and looked around.

Before he knew it, Max had no idea where he was, and he wasn't sure about how he could find his way home. Confused and tired, Max turned back the way he came.

Only, he couldn't remember where he had turned and where he had gone straight. He was so worried about finding John that he forgot to concentrate on where he was, and now he had no idea.

Max was lost.

Desperate to go back home to see whether John had returned, Max started trying to follow his smell to see if he could get home that way.

Only, the harder he tried, the harder it was for him to seek out his smell.

The sweet smell of supper served in the houses around him made him feel depressed. For a moment, he thought about what it would be like for the other dogs, cats, and even people whose suppers are now being served to them. They would be relaxing and enjoying an exquisite evening.

Max grew terrified as he worried that he would never make it home to enjoy a meal with John. By this time, he didn't even know if John could find him, either.

But Max made up his mind to find his home, so he kept jogging and trying to seek out the familiar path. At one point, a person with dark hair like John's walked by, and Max thought maybe it had been him, but it wasn't. Feeling sad, Max just kept on jogging.

He jogged even faster when he heard the person behind him start talking because he worried that they might be dangerous.

By now, it was beginning to get dark, and Max was getting very scared.

He had no idea where John was, and he felt sad that he couldn't find him. It couldn't get any worse because he couldn't even see his own house yet.

Finally, Max grew tired and laid underneath a tree on someone's lawn and tried to nod off.

He hoped that perhaps he would awaken and realize that it was all just a terrible dream.

Sometime later, when the road lights turned on and the sky was black and filled with stars, Max heard something in the distance. It sounded as if maybe, just maybe, someone was calling his name, but Max wasn't sure about what he heard.

He lay still a little longer, but with his head high and at alert.

Then, he heard it again.

This time, he was sure that he heard someone call his name.

He jumped up and began running toward the sound.

The sound, however, was coming from someone who was not John.

Afraid, Max slunk away and tried to distance himself from the stranger calling his name. Still, the person wanted to call him forward. Max refused to budge, though.

A few minutes later, after the person kept trying to get close to Max, another voice came piercing through the night.

This time, Max was sure it had been John! He got excited and immediately ran toward the voice, and it was John!

Standing in the night, John was there with Max's leash in hand and a pocket filled with cookies to spare!

Max grew so excited that he jumped everywhere and leapt right into John's arms. He jumped so hard; John almost fell over!

John was so pleased to find Max, that he gave him plenty of strokes and hugs and let Max lick him everywhere on the face in excitement. John attached Max's leash, and together they walked home, and John gave Max many, many treats. On their walk home, things were very different.

Because it was dark now, everyone was asleep.

Now, Hopper was gone and nowhere to be found.

She was probably away, sleeping together with her family.

Willy's bed was empty in the window, and he was nowhere to be seen.

He was probably upstairs in bed together with his family, getting his belly rubbed and preparing to nod off for the night.

And Liza, well, she was inside someone's house sleeping in the window!

Max was so shocked to find out that Liza lived across the road from him and didn't just sleep in the bushes where he always saw her playing and napping. He tried to get her attention, but she was sound asleep in her bed and would not wake. As they arrived home, John brought Max inside and gave him another big hug and strokes.

Then, he gave Max an additional special dog treat and let him cuddle on the couch while they watched evening television.

At bedtime, John let Max sleep in his bed instead of leaving him to sleep in his own bed on the ground.

He was so happy to have Max home that he just wanted to hold him and cuddle him after a long day of getting lost and trying to find his way home again.

Max was so happy to be home, he fell sound asleep in John's arms, snoring and dreaming about his adventure in the neighborhood.

The Princess And The Frog

There once lived a Princess who didn't behave like the kind of Princess we hear of. She wanted to play alone in the palace gardens with her favorite glowing golden ball.

The difficulty with playing alone was that no one was ever there to get the ball if she threw it too high. One day, as she was going around lilies, daisies, and roses, she threw her ball higher than she had ever before.

Her beautiful golden ball had plopped directly into a lake close by! She visited the lake and watched sadly as the golden circle sank further and further into the water. The Princess looked down at her dress. She was wearing her favorite golden dress; the shimmers and diamonds on the bodice of the elegant outfit were rare, and she was nervous about the likelihood that if she entered the water, she would ruin her dress. Upset by her circumstance, the Princess began to cry.

Suddenly, the Princess heard a weird commotion originating from the other side of the lake.

She hid behind some nearby bushes and watched as a little Boy talked to an older woman. The Princess had never seen either of them before, but she felt that she wasn't obliged to take note of their conversation. "I can offer you anything you desire!" said the old woman, "I can cause you to be small, I can cause you to be grown, I can even cause you to be something out of nothing!"

The little Boy seemed very excited and proceeded to make a wish. The Princess didn't hear what he asked for, but she saw a woosh of mist and smoke, and suddenly the little Boy had disappeared! The older woman then cackled and laughed at what she had done. It was then that The Princess realized that she must be a Witch!

The Princess looked all around and saw that no one else had seen what had happened. She considered her ball at the bottom of the lake and her beautiful golden dress and decided that she would ask the Witch to retrieve her ball from the lake.

As she walked towards the Witch, she saw a little Frog jump clumsily into the lake and giggled. It was at this moment that the witch heard her and turned.

"Hello, child," said the Witch, "Have you come to make a wish?" "Oh, I would like to!" replied the Princess.

"Good! I can offer you anything you desire!" said the old woman, "I can cause you to be small, I can cause you to be grown, I can even cause you to be something out of nothing!"

"Oh, I only wish for one thing," replied the Princess. "You see when I play with my favorite ball alone in the garden and when I throw it up far too high, and it lands in this lake, it sinks to the bottom. I could go retrieve it myself, but my dress is expensive and covered in rare gemstones. I would hate to ruin it with the dirty lake water!" "Very well!" said the Witch, "I must warn you, however, that magic comes at a great price. What are you going give me in return for retrieving your ball and sparing that pretty dress of yours?"

The Princess stood and thought. She was sure that if she asked her Father to offer something to the Witch, he would say no. She didn't know it was worth the trouble –she could just get herself a new ball.

She couldn't give her the dress as that was far too precious to her. Finally, she had the right idea.

"What if I gave you a lock of my golden hair?" she asked, "It's gorgeous!"

The Witch smiled to herself. "A lock of your golden hair would be perfect, my child. Just allow me to chop it off..." Suddenly, a little brown Frog leapt out from the tree they were standing by and landed on the old Witch's face. The Frog then yelled to the small Princess, "Run! She is not going to give you what you want. She only wishes to steal your riches!"

Surprised, the small Princess ran to get far away from the crazy brown Frog and, therefore, the mean old witch.

"Well, this just won't do," thought the Princess to herself, "now how will I get my ball?"

Just then, another little spring Frog that had bounced clumsily into the lake before came hopping up to her feet.

Jump! Jump! Bounce!

"Hello, little Frog. I don't suppose you know how I could get my ball from the bottom of the lake, do you?" She said to the Frog.

He sighed, "Well, can't you swim?"

Shocked and a little offended, the Princess replied, "Well, in fact, I can swim! I just don't want to ruin my beautiful and expensive dress!"

"Very well," he replied, "I suppose I could get it for you, but first, I need to ask you a favor."

The Princess had nearly had it with payments and favors by now, so she almost refused. On the other hand, she realized just how harmless a little Frog is, and she figured he couldn't hurt her.

"I suppose, what is it that want?" she asked the Frog.

"Nothing, except for you to play with me," he answered.

The Princess thought this over. She could use somebody to play with, and without this Frog, she may never get her ball back - but also, what kind of fun can playing with a frog be? Deciding that he would eventually get bored after a while, she agreed.

The Frog leapt into the lake and swam quickly to the bottom. When he arose, he held the small Princess's golden ball in one hand.

With excitement beaming all over her face having gotten back her ball; she ran over to the Frog and gave him a quick kiss on the crown of his head.

Suddenly there was a whoosh of mist and smoke, and the little Frog suddenly became the small boy she had seen lecture the witch across the lake earlier!

"Why you're not a frog at all! You're a boy!" She exclaimed.

"Indeed," He replied, with a little of relief in his voice, "I was trying to get a wish from a Witch to find a lover when she turned me into a frog and stole my Prince's crown! As soon as I saw you having a conversation with her, I had to possess that other frog to stop you so she wouldn't trick you as well."

"Oh my!" shrieked the Princess, "How could I even have been so absentminded? Because of you, my day has been saved twice!"

"I was happy as well!" replied the Prince, "I hope you're still willing to keep your promise and spend the day playing with me? I'm afraid I've been lonely and could use a companion." "Of course!" replied the Princess.

And so they spent the remainder of that day playing together with the Princess's favorite ball. Later that day, he saw the Witch sneaking around the Prince's castle with the Prince's stolen crown, she was caught and put in jail, and the Prince got his crown back. The two friends enjoyed playing together for the remainder of their days.

The Bear Feast

The Old Man was miserable. His friends and family were long gone. He began to contemplate whether he should leave the village and start another life elsewhere. "If I lived somewhere new, I would not need to keep thinking about being lonely anymore," he thought. Still, he stressed, "If I'm going away to a different village and the people there see that I'm alone, they'll think that I needed to escape from my home village because I was accused of some shocking crimes." Instead, he thought that he would explore and sleep in the backwoods away from anyone else.

The Old Man was so tragic, voyaging alone in the forested areas, it occurred to him to travel to the bears and quickly let the bears eat him. The bear village was by an outsized salmon creek, so he headed toward the river in the first part of the day until he found a bear trail, and he sat down at its end. He felt that when the Bears came out along this path, they might see him, which would be the end of him.

Before long, as he lay there, he heard the brambles breaking. Then, countless grizzly bears came along. The foremost, massive Bear led the rest, and the tips of his hair were white. Then, the Old Man got scared. Out of nowhere, he now knew that he wouldn't like to die at all, and certainly not by Bears. So when the leader of the Bears came up to him, the older man stood up. He said: "I have come to welcome you to a feast."

At that, the leading Bear's hair stood straight up. The older man thought that he would be no more. But he spoke again, this time saying, "I have come to welcome you to a feast, but if you're planning to murder me, I will go on from here. I'm separated from everyone else. I have lost everything, including my family and my friends."

When he said this, the leading Bear rotated and snarled to the bears that were following. Then, the gathering of them turned back the way they had come. Eventually, the Old Man turned and walked toward his village quickly. He considered whether the leading Bear had told the other bears behind him to return and prepare because he invited them to a feast.

"Well, if that's how it is, I better prepare to host a feast," thought the Old Man. When he returned home, he began to tidy up his place. He removed the old sand around the chimney and replaced it with clean sand. Then, he went to pick up some wood. When he mentioned to the others in the village what he was doing and why they were all shocked, they said to him: "Why did you do something like that? The grizzlies are our enemies. You do not want grizzly bears in your home." When he came back home, the Old Man removed his shirt and painted his chest. He put stripes of red over his upper arm muscles, a red line over his heart and another over the top of his chest.

He was prepared; he stood outside of the doorway trying to find his bears at the start of the day. At long last, he saw them at the mouth of the brook, led by the largest Bear, the one with white hair on its tips. When the other village people saw the bears, they were frightened to such an extent that they shut themselves in their houses. Still, the Old Man stood by his doorway to greet his visitors. He invited them into the home and gave them seats, setting the leader Bear in the center at the rear of the house and the rest around him.

First, he served them an oversized plate of cranberries dressed in oil. The biggest Bear seemed to express something to his friends, and when he began to eat, the rest began to eat, as well. They watched him and mimicked him. The host next served a salmon dish, sprinkling clover weed and dandelion on top for seasoning. Then, a plate of deer meat with pine nuts. For dessert, was raspberries with nectar.

After they were through, the massive Bear seemed to converse together with his host for some extra time. It had been as if the bear was telling him a story, for he would gaze toward the smoke gap from time to time even as he was talking. When finished, he headed toward his host and licked the paint from his arm and chest. And each of the other bears did likewise. The Old Man felt as if he was having his troubles licked away.

The day after this had occurred, the tiniest Bear returned to the Old Man's house in human form and addressed him.

"He born to a human being," he told the Old Man, "but had been caught and raised by the bears." (Do you mean "I was born to a human being" "but was caught…")

The Bear-Man asked the Old Man if he had understood their leader, and he answered, "No."

"He was letting you recognize," the Bear-Man answered, "that he's in a similar situation as you. That he, as well, is old and has lost all of his friends. He had heard of you before seeing you, he said. He instructed you to think about him when you are grieving for your lost ones, as he understands how it feels."

When the Old Man asked the Bear-Man why he had not told him that day when the bears were at the feast, he answered that he wasn't permitted to transform into his human form and communicate in his local language while the bear leader was near.

After this, whenever the village people gave a banquet, they would always welcome an enemy to the party. And that they would become friends, because the Old Man had done so with the leader of the bears.

The Bear And The Travelers

Two travelers were walking through the forest. They had vowed before they started the journey together to help each other if they met any danger on their way.

Not long into the journey, they suddenly faced a Bear.

The first Traveler didn't keep his promise. He climbed up a tree forgetting about his travel companion.

The second Traveler did not know how to climb a tree, but he knew that confronting a Bear was a terrible idea.

He thought for a second about what to do, and immediately, he fell on his back. He was playing dead.

The Bear approached him. It smelt him and left, thinking that he was dead.

After the Bear left, the traveler on the treetop asked the other one who lay on the ground, "What did the Bear tell you?"

"Do not accept a companion who leaves you in your time of trouble," said the second Traveler.

David Goes To See The Whales

Have you ever imagined what it might be like to go out to the ocean with your family to watch the whales play?

Whale watching is a beautiful experience that is enjoyed by many that live near the gorgeous ocean.

In tonight's story, we talk about David and his whale adventures with his family, and every one of the beautiful experiences he had, and the emotions he experienced along the way.

Before we start our story, be sure that you are ready for bed!

Say goodnight to your family, brush your teeth, and grab a drink of water.

If you've got a favorite blanket or stuffed animal, snuggle up close with them and get ready for an exquisite night's sleep.

Then, once you are ready, we will spend a couple of minutes breathing to unwind with a relaxing meditation before starting tonight's story.

That way, your body is relaxed and prepared to remain still while you hear the story and prepare yourself for a lovely dream.

For this breathing meditation, we are getting to inhale to the count of five, hold it for two seconds, and then exhale to the count of seven.

This exercise helps you to relax your mind, and it tells your body that it's time to settle down and go to sleep.

You can start this meditation once you are ready by breathing to the count of one, two, three, four, five, holding it for one, two, and exhalation for one, two, three, four, five, six, and seven.

Again, inhale for one, two, three, four, five, hold it for one, two, and exhale for one, two, three, four, five, six, seven.

Breathe in again for one, two, three, four, five, hold it for one, two, and exhale for one, two, three, four, five, six, seven.

Breathe in for one, two, three, four, five, hold your breath for one, two, and let it out for two, three, four, five, six, seven.

One more time, inhale for one, two, three, four, five, hold it for one, two, and let it choose (exhale for?) one, two, three, four, five, six, and seven.

Now, let your breath return to normal as you listen to this fantastic story about David and his whale watching experience.

David was so excited to travel with his family to the coast.

He spent the entire week packing his bags.

He packed his pants, shirts, underwear, socks, shoes, and even a couple of his favorite toys.

He packed his toothbrush, toothpaste, shampoo, conditioner, and a little towel in a smaller bag.

All of his bags were ready on Friday morning when it was time for him and his parents to make the drive to the coast where they would stay with David's grandparents for the weekend.

David was so excited to see his grandparents as he had not seen them in months, and he missed them dearly.

The whole way there, he excitedly talked about what they might do, how they might spend their time, and what fun it might be to spend the weekend together with his grandparents.

To help him contain his excitement, his parents encouraged him to play games like counting how many telephone poles he saw in one town and counting how many green cars he saw along the way.

David played along and counted out 19 telephone poles and 37 green cars.

After what felt like forever, David and his parents got to the coast and his grandparents' house.

His grandparents were as excited to see him as he was to see them and they enjoyed an exquisite evening eating his Grandma's delicious spaghetti and meatballs with a slice of cake for dessert.

That night, he slept in the guest room with a big grin on his face. He was so excited to be with his grandparents again.

When morning came, David woke up and saw that his grandparents and parents were packing some bags.

"Are we leaving already?" David frowned.

"No, not at all. We are going on an adventure today!" David's Grandpa exclaimed. "An adventure? Where?" David asked.

"It's a surprise." His Grandpa grinned.

"Before the journey, you should have a good breakfast to help you start your day!

Come on! Let's enjoy some pancakes and bacon before we leave." David's Grandma said, calling everyone into the dining room.

Everyone went and ate their breakfast, and it was delicious.

When they finished having breakfast, they cleaned their plates and got ready to leave.

"Is it time for the journey now?" David asked.

"It sure is!" his Grandpa grinned, giving him a thumbs up.

David, his parents, and his grandparents all got their shoes on and left the house. On their way, David had mixed feelings of excitement and confusion.

He had no idea what they were doing, but he knew that he had to make the most it because he always had a good time with his grandparents.

As they drove, David began to see the ocean ahead of them.

He could see it getting more significant and more prominent as they drove closer.

"Are we going to the beach?" He asked.

"Sort of." His Mom said, keeping their adventure a mystery.

David grew even more curious as they drove closer and closer to the beach and eventually parked in a parking zone near the water.

"We are going to the beach, aren't we?" He said, excited.

"You'll see." His Dad grinned.

His parents and grandparents picked up several pieces of luggage out of the trunk and locked the car as they began walking toward a building on the beach.

When they got there, David saw plenty of pictures and statues of whales on the walls inside.

"What are we doing, Grandpa?" He asked, looking around in wonder.

"We're going whale watching!" His Grandpa revealed.

"Whale watching? I have never experienced this before! I am so excited!" David said, jumping all around.

His parents and grandparents smiled as they watched him, and everybody got ready to go whale watching.

When they were all checked in, one of the guides led David and his family to the boat that they would board.

David and his family got aboard and sat down to watch the vast sea.

David was so excited about what was happening that he could hardly contain himself, but the whale watching Guide told him it was vital that he sit down and stay still so he didn't hurt himself or fall off the boat accidentally.

The Guide gave each of them a life jacket a moment later and told them what to do if anything went wrong.

He assured them that it was unlikely that anyone would fall out but it was vital that he tells them what to do just in case.

As David listened to the guide, he looked over the boat's edge and realized how deep the water was.

He began to grow scared as he realized what might happen if he moved, so he sat completely still.

He sat so still that David's Grandma wondered if something was wrong.

"Are you okay?" she asked.

"I am, I'm just frightened of falling into the water. I have never fallen into the ocean before, what if I get hurt?" he asked.

"You are going to be okay, just stay relaxed and stay with grandpa and me, and we will keep you safe." David's Dad assured him.

He was sitting between his Dad and Grandpa, and, realizing that he wasn't alone, he began to feel at ease.

For the first few minutes out on the water, David still felt scared.

He worried that something might happen that would hurt them.

After they had been out for a short time, though, David began to calm down.

He relaxed so much that he was ready to tease his Grandpa with jokes as they enjoyed the view and had a great time together.

Soon, they made it to the place where the whales were, and the Guide told them to look up.

David looked out where the Guide was pointing and saw the whales' backs as they bobbed through the water.

They appeared to be playing and dancing in the waves as they swam around.

One even sprayed water up into the air above their boat!

The Guide carefully moved the boat a little closer so that they might get a better view.

David was surprised by how beautiful and exciting the whales were to observe.

When he asked to travel closer, the Guide told him that they had to remain at a distance so that the whales didn't get hurt.

The Guide said that sometimes the whales became so interested in the boats that they might touch them with their noses and get hurt by the propellers.

David didn't want the whales to get hurt, so he agreed they should keep their distance and enjoy the whales from afar.

They sat there for a short time and watched the whales dancing in the waves as they enjoyed the daylight.

It seemed as if they were all playing together, and David thought that was cute.

After a little while, the whales began to disappear.

The other boats that had also been whale watching began to go back toward shore, and their Guide suggested that David's family also started going back.

"Aw, but I don't want to! I'm having fun!" David said.

"I know, but we've got to say goodbye to the pod of whales and allow them to have a nice sleep!" David's Mom said.

"What is a pod of whales?"

"A pod is a gathering of whales." His Mom answered.

"Oh. Bye pod of whales!" David said, waving at the whales.

The Guide began to take David and his family back to shore.

When they got there, they took their life jackets off and got off the boat one by one.

His parents went to ask the Guide some questions while David and his grandparents brought their bags back to the car.

When his parents finished talking, all of them got into the car and began to go back to his grandparent's house.

Slowly, the ocean grew further and further away as they went back toward the suburbs where his grandparents lived.

Before he knew it, they were back home and prepared to enjoy a delicious dinner together.

David was tired, but he stayed awake long enough to enjoy dinner with his grandparents and family.

When dinner was ready, they all sat down together at the table and enjoyed an exquisite meal.

They had ham, mashed potatoes, carrots, gravy, corn, and buns.

After that, David and his family enjoyed another slice of his favorite cake for dessert. David even got to have a couple of the cookies his Grandma often ate together with her tea after dinner.

As they were sitting down enjoying the evening, his Grandma asked: "David, what was your favorite part of the day?"

"My favorite part was seeing the pod of whales playing in the waves. It seemed like they were dancing! And when the whale sprayed water into the air!" David said, making a grand gesture into the air as if he were the whale spraying water.

David's parents and grandparents giggled as they watched him act out the whales. When he has done, David sat down on the couch and started to nod off.

"Are you tired?" his Mom asked.

"Yes," David whispered.

David's Dad carried him to the guest room and tucked him in so that he could enjoy a sweet night's sleep after a fantastic day of whale watching together with his family. The end!

Going on adventures are often fun, but it can also sometimes be scary.

When you don't know what you're doing, it is often scary to try new things.

The good thing is, you do not need to go on adventures alone, and you'll always have your loved ones to assist you in feeling safe.

When you know that you will be safe while on an adventure, adventures are often great fun and may create wonderful lifelong memories.

You may not know it now, but these memories are going to be very special to you!

As you test out new adventures in your own life, I encourage you to keep these affirmations accessible to assist you to feel confident when embarking on adventures:

"It is safe to travel on adventures."

"Adventures with my family are fun."

"Trying new things is great."

"I feel my feelings when I try new things."

"Adventure is fun."

"I love adventures with my family."

"I hear the principles once I continue adventures."

"Listening to the principles helps me stay safe."

"Adventures are often an excellent time."

"These memories will last forever."

Deer In The Wood

One day a deer was born. His name was Oliver. His Mom washed him down together with her tongue.

"Oliver," she said, "my little Oliver."

The young Oliver was curious about everything. He learned he was a deer, as was his Mom. He realized there are other deer in the forest, and someday he would meet them. He knew the deer made the trail his Mom followed. Bugs and critters, sounds, and smells — so many wonders to observe!

Sometimes on a path, suddenly, his Mom would stop still. She would open her ears wide and listen from all around. Oliver would pause and await the signal from his Mom. Finally, when she said, "It's OK, there is no danger! We can go," then both of them would begin walking again. But he didn't know why they needed to stop.

His Mom took him to the mountain clearing but then she hopped directly ahead of him. "Stop!" she said. "Stay here. I should go first. Stay until I call you. But if I begin to run, you ought to turn and run back to the forested area very quickly. Try not to stop. Do you understand me?" Oliver's Mom slowly ventured out far away from the hidden trees. She sniffed all around. Finally, she called, "It's OK, Oliver, nothing to worry about. Please!" He walked carefully to meet her.

Goodness, what a splendid sun! Back in the forested areas, Oliver had seen a wandering sunbeam once in a while, but here, the gorgeous sweltering sun warmed him all over. He felt beautiful and bounced high into the air. Whenever he landed on grass, he would bounce back, again and again.

In certain spots, the flowers were so thick and that they made a sweet carpet. But what was that tiny thing moving all around? "See, Mother!" said Oliver. "The flower is flying." That flower sure did move a lot. Oliver thought that it had broken from its stem to rise and move all around like that.

"That isn't a flower, Oliver," said his Mother, "It's a butterfly."

At that time – crack, crack, crack! On a stone was a youthful squirrel, jumping up and down.

"Hi, there! My name is Sally," smiled the squirrel, raising one tiny paw. "Want to play?" "Sure!" said Oliver.

"Catch me!" Sally jumped off the stone into the grass, ceaselessly bouncing. Oliver was somewhat quicker at running and hopping, but Sally was better at hiding away, so both made some good memories.

On the flowers, a spiky ball was sliding over to them. "Why I'd know those spikes anywhere!" said Sally. "It's my friend, Paul. He's a porcupine, and he's under the flowers. Paul?" And indeed, a spiky little head sprung up.

"This is Oliver," said Sally. Soon, the three of them were investigating the clearing, sniffing its rich, profound scents.

Eventually, Sally and Paul needed to travel home. Oliver looked around. "Mother! Where are you?" He saw her at the furthest side of the valley, with an animal that looked a bit like her.

"Oliver, come meet my sister Ella and her two little ones!" Oliver's Mom exclaimed. Oliver bounced over. Two fawns, little Sienna and her sister Daisy were running all around their Mom's legs.

Sienna gave a jump and landed right ahead of Oliver, then hopped back to Daisy. Carefully, Oliver ventured up to her. Sienna jumped alongside, and Daisy followed. Soon, the three of them were chasing one another here and there in the grass.

"Now escape and play, all of you," said Oliver's Mom.

From that time on, the three young deer played and yelled. They ran and chased each other and ate strawberries and blueberries in the bushes. Sometimes, they only talked. One time, Oliver asked, "Do you recognize what danger means?" "Something awful," murmured Daisy.

"But what is it?" asked Oliver.

"I know what danger is," said Sienna, "It's what you run from." But soon, they were chasing and playing once again.

Oliver's Mom and Ella came up. "Please, children," they said, "It's time to go home."

Far away at the very top point of a slope, two large deer came into view, with large heads of antlers. Looking at them, Sienna asked, "Who are they?" "Those are your Dad's," said Ella.

"If you're careful and do not run into any danger," said Oliver's Mom to her child, "Someday you'll get older and as big and handsome as your Dad. And you'll have antlers, as well." Oliver beamed.

As Oliver grew, he found out the way to sniff the air. He could tell if his friend Sally was coming or if a fox had recently run by. He could tell if it might rain soon too.

One evening there was an enormous thunderstorm. Lightning flashed, and thunder smashed. Oliver thought the planet was ending. But, when he lay by his Mom's side, he felt safe.

When Oliver was wandering about in the forested area, he smelt a sharp, unsavory smell. Curious, he followed it. It led to a clearing, where a weird creature stood. He had never seen such a beast. It could get up on its back legs and everyone four of its legs. It was covered in black fur and sniffed at the air while grunting. The smell of the creature filled him with dread. The beast raised its long black arm. Quickly, Oliver's Mom ran up to him.

"Run, Oliver, run! As fast as you can!"

Oliver's Mom leapt over bushes and fallen trees. He kept up with her until they were back at their quiet home. Afterwards, Oliver's Mom asked, "Did you see the Bear?" Oliver nodded, yes. "That is the animal that brings danger," she said, and both of them shivered.

Oliver was all the while growing. The first time he woke to find his Mom gone from his side, he was scared. It was early morning and still dark. "Mother! Mother!" he called out. An oversized shadow drew nearer, much larger than his Mother's. Standing in a pool of moonlight, an excellent old Buck looked stern and harsh.

"Why are you calling?" asked the Buck with a glare. "Aren't you ready to look out for yourself?" Oliver didn't answer. He lowered his head in shame. "Look up," said the old Buck, "Listen, watch, smell, and look out for yourself.

You will be fine on your own."

As time went by, the leaves changed, and Oliver grew even more prominent.

His Mom began leaving him alone for longer and longer, letting him meet other deer and animals in the forest. Sienna, Daisy, Sally, and Paul were still Oliver's closest friends. But he also found different creatures interesting to observe and sometimes fun to play with.

One wet winter day, the awful smell of Bears came to visit the forest. The smell was so strong that there must be many Bears having a gathering! Most animals immediately fled due to the threat. But some weren't as fortunate. The Bear's uproarious commotion and incredible force killed many animals, one of which was Ella, Oliver's Mom's sister.

After that awful day, Oliver felt lost. He wandered about. How could this terrible thing have happened? Suddenly, the good old Buck ventured out before him.

"Were you at the glade when it happened?" the old Buck asked.

"Yes," said Oliver.

"Do you know if Daisy and Sienna are OK without their Mom?" asked the old Buck.

Understanding what the Buck was implying, Oliver felt suddenly strong. "I can look out for myself!" he said, looking up.

The great old Buck smiled. "Listen," he said. "Smell. Watch. Find out the way to live and take care. Be on the lookout for yourself, now goodbye." And he evaporated into the deep forest.

Winter came. A robust and severe cold moved through the forested area. Deep snow coated the forest floor. There was little or no food to eat. Oliver constantly felt hungry and cold. Most of the bark on the trees had been stripped away by hungry deer. The cold wind raged on, still.

Daisy was more petite than Oliver and Sienna, so she shivered constantly. She could hardly stand upright anymore.

One day a gathering of crows flew overhead, shouting noisily. "Caw! Caw!" The geese also screamed in the sky, "Look! Look!" they warned them about the Bears coming - once again!

Sally jumped here and there anxiously. "We're surrounded! They're everywhere!" A solitary roar smashed like hell, and one rabbit yelped nearby. All the animals ran everywhere, even the tiny titmouse. Large black paws appeared and another howl rang out. Roar! Roar!

Sally called out to Oliver, "We've got to leave!" Oliver and Sally began to run away. But was that Daisy, lying in the snow?

"Daisy!" said Oliver.

"I fell," said Daisy. "I'm too weak. You go on, Oliver." Oliver hesitated.

"Oliver, run! Don't just stand there, run!" He took off, and as Oliver ran along, he called behind him, "I will return for you, Daisy!" Oliver ran and ran. Soon, the roars began to die out.

When Oliver went back to where Daisy had been, there was no sign of her, not even her tracks. Sienna was walking around the spot. "What happened to her?" she howled. But they both knew that a Bear had taken Daisy away.

After weeks, finally, little blades of the latest green grass sprung up through the snow, and then, an ever-increasing number of tufts of green. After what was left of the snow had melted away, Oliver could feel the heaviness of his quickly developing antlers.

As the trees and bushes gradually became green and the weather warmed, all the animals began to act so strangely. Birds fluttered about in pairs. Numerous creatures, large and tiny, went two by two. His friend Paul invested all his energy into a girl porcupine and scarcely saw Oliver. Even his friend Sally was everlastingly gazing at a young man squirrel and bouncing up and down.

"What's happened to my friends?" asked Oliver. "I am separated from everyone else." There was a stirring in the meadow behind him. There stood Sienna, but she was grown up now, as was he. All of them were thinking, "How different you look!" They checked each other out and smiled.

"It's been a long time since we've seen each other," said Sienna.

"Yes, I know," said Oliver. They discussed their memories. "Do you remember playing tag in the glade?" asked one.

"Do you remember all the berries on the bushes we ate?" asked the other. The two got along splendidly. A fat deer came up to them, sniffing the air.

"Sister, don't you recognize me?"

Sienna and Oliver turned in amazement. "Daisy!" They ran up to her in happiness.

"No doubt about it!" said Oliver.

"Where have you been?" asked Sienna.

Daisy recounted her story. "I was with a Bear. I have seen more of them." They had found her where she rested in the snow and carried her to where they lived. "It was as cozy as summer inside," said Daisy. "Rain may pour outside, but not inside the cave where the Bears live. It's always warm and dry! They also had tons of food stored up for the winter - turnips, lettuce, potatoes, and carrots - yum!" "Weren't you scared, though?" asked Sienna.

"No, the Bear wouldn't hurt me. If they look after you, or if you serve them, they're good to you," said Daisy. "They all cared on behalf of me there. The Cubs loved playing with me."

One day when Daisy and Oliver were together, they smelt the smell of a Bear. "We should hide, quickly!" said Oliver. "No need for that," said Daisy. "Bears know me." She wandered over to where the Bears were, and suddenly one roared and swiped one giant paw, scratching Daisy! Daisy stumbled away, running as fast as she could while wounded.

Luckily, the Bear never came after Daisy. Instead, when the smell of the Bear left, Oliver pulled his friend to a secure spot where she could rest and be free from danger. Oliver remembered what weeds his mom used to eat to fix an injury quicker. As he carried the plants to Daisy, he wondered, "Why does this always happen?" Oliver thought of the good old Buck, who had stated, "See for yourself." See what?

Sienna and Oliver's Mom carried Daisy's food and chatted together with her for quite a while. Oliver frequently dropped by, as well, until Daisy got better. The words from the good Old Buck were still fresh in his head – "Figure out the way to live and take care." Oliver was starting to understand.

Seasons changed, and Oliver grew still taller. His antlers were almost fully developed now. One day, Oliver found another smell around. It was a hot and smoky smell. A herd of crows hurried ahead, cawing boisterously. "Fire! Fire!"

Quickly, the animals were running as fast as possible. It had been hard to run from the flames as they came from everywhere. Nighttime went by with fire and smoke; as the sun started peeking above the horizon, the flames finally began to hamper. The smell of the fire was disappearing, as well.

The great old Buck stood before Oliver. His head was grey now. Still, he bore his antlers with satisfaction. "Come with me," he said kindly. "I've got to show you something before I go."

He led Oliver through the forested areas to an abandoned cave. Along with the smell of the fire was the horrendous smell of Bears that had sent perpetual fear to their souls.

"Try not to be scared," the old Buck said. They visited a particular cave. "See, Oliver," he said. Standing a little distance away from what used to be a cave. It was burned down all around the entrance and on the inside too. The cave was now vacant.

"Oliver," said the old Buck. "The homes of the Bears got burned by fire just bit like the places where we stay in the forested area. Bears aren't above us. We are the same. Do you understand what I am saying, Oliver?"

"Fire consumes the forested area where we live, and it consumes the caves of Bears, as well," said Oliver. "We aren't all that different from Bears."

"We both sleep in the same forest," said the good old Buck.

"Yes," Oliver said.

"I can go now," the old Buck said. "Try not to follow me. My time has come. Goodbye, my child, I like you so."

Now Oliver had become an enormous buck himself. His antlers sparkled and shined in the sun.

Sometimes he would visit the parts of the forested areas where he had spent his youth. Some of the trails were still there. Once while wandering there, he saw Daisy and her sister, Sienna. When he saw Sienna, his heartbeat quickened. He wanted to run to her. He took to her and that they had a few fawns together. At some point, she left them alone for a period of time. Then, he heard the cries of two little fawns.

"Mother! Mother!" they called.

"Would you be ready to look out for yourselves?" asked Oliver. The siblings searched Oliver in wonderment. The older one replied, "Well, I can look out for my sister!" Oliver liked the young fawn. He helped him find the young face he used to see when he looked in the stream years ago.

"Listen to me," said Oliver to the two fawns. "You should pay attention, and you smell the air. See for yourself. You'll be fine on your own."

In A Rabbit Hole

Lisa always loved reading. She read before school and after school, and at the weekend. Her friends called her a bookworm. Lisa didn't mind being called a bookworm. She enjoyed it because it gave her all the more excuse to take a seat and skim.

One day Lisa was reading in the garden. She was reading a book called Alice in Wonderland. She had read it before, but she loved the characters in the story. Lisa especially loved the White Rabbit. She wondered what it might be like to follow a rabbit down his hole as Alice did. It had been quite a hot day when Lisa was reading her book. Lisa lent back on the trunk where she was sitting and fell asleep. Suddenly she awakened to a pattering sound.

Lisa slowly opened one eye first and then the other. Then she rubbed both eyes to check she wasn't seeing things. She saw a Rabbit, a White Rabbit hopping ahead of her. Lisa couldn't believe this sight. The White Rabbit stopped ahead of Lisa and began to shake its head. It had a thorough look at Lisa and began to speak.

"Excuse me, little girl," said the White Rabbit. Lisa just sat together with her mouth open and stared. "Excuse me, little girl, will you lead me to the closest rabbit hole?" asked the White Rabbit. Lisa shook her head. She had not seen a rabbit burrow in the garden.

"Well, you're a silly girl," said the Rabbit. It tutted annoyingly and began to steer off.

Lisa didn't want to be called silly by a rabbit, so she called after it.

"Sorry, Rabbit, perhaps I can assist you in searching for one?" suggested Lisa.

The Rabbit stopped for a moment, then nodded its head and beckoned for her to follow.

Lisa wasn't sure about following the Rabbit, but follow him, she did. Then suddenly, the Rabbit disappeared and then so did Lisa. She felt the world falling beneath her. Down and down fell Lisa, and eventually, she landed with a bump.

Many little bunnies were running along the track that led ahead of her. All the rabbits had small bags on their backs, and they were in a hurry. Finally, Lisa managed to stop one of the rabbits.

"Where are you going?" asked Lisa.

The little Rabbit was quite out of breath. "We are off to high school. Come on; otherwise, you are going to be late," said the Rabbit. Lisa looked very surprised. Rabbits are going to school! She decided to follow the rabbits because she didn't know what else to try to do. All the small rabbits ran to the gates of an enormous school. They saw the varsity yard as the bell rang for lessons to start.

Little rabbits lined up, and a Giant Rabbit came to the varsity stairs' highest point. "Hop on, everyone," said the Giant Rabbit. Everyone went hopping along the corridors to get to their classrooms. Lisa followed along too. She didn't jump. She just walked along slowly and located a desk to sit at.

She was sitting next to an annoying rabbit that kept tapping its foot on the ground under the desk. Then Lisa heard a loud crunching noise behind her. She turned round to see a rabbit munching on a carrot. This was turning into a crazy classroom.

The first lesson was about Boadicea, the Bunny Queen, who led a military against the Romans. Lisa couldn't believe her eyes at an image of a rabbit riding a chariot on the history book's first page.

"You see, rabbits made history! We were a part of the first battles against the enemy, the Romans," said the Teacher. Lisa tried to concentrate, but the lesson was on; the rabbits in the classroom were misbehaving and not listening. They were munching on carrots and eating lettuce leaves. Eventually, it was time for a lunch break. Lisa went outside with all the bunnies. She wondered what they might do during their recess time.

It was time to play hopscotch. Lisa nodded her head as she saw all the bunnies hopping in the hopscotch games. Suddenly Lisa saw the Rabbit she had followed. He was anxiously crossing the playground. Lisa decided she should follow him because she didn't know how she would get back home. It had been all alright to follow a rabbit down a rabbit burrow, but Lisa decided it was time for this adventure to come to an end. She caught up with the Rabbit and tapped him politely on his shoulder. He turned around and checked her out with a puzzled expression.

"Excuse me," said Lisa politely. "Can you help me find the way back to my garden?" "Well, if you would like to travel back.

You have to travel backwards. Walk backwards the way you came," said the Rabbit.

Lisa looked puzzled at that concept. She had no choice but to follow the Rabbit as it began to lead her backwards. She hoped that it took her home. She was so busy walking backwards that she didn't notice she had seen something else on the trail, the trail back home to her garden.

"Ouch!" came a touching voice. Lisa looked everywhere, but she couldn't see anything. She knew that she had to keep walking when she heard the tiny voice again.

"What are you doing walking backwards?" asked the voice.

"I am trying to get back home to my garden," answered Lisa.

"Well, why don't you turn around and walk normally?" said the voice.

Lisa looked down again, and on the trail, she saw a wiggly worm. The worm had tiny spectacles on the top of its nose and had a book under its front legs. "Hi. I'm Billy Bookworm," said the worm as it looked at Lisa.

Lisa looked down, amazed. "Was there such a thing as a bookworm?" she wondered. There should be a bookworm in this strange place. Lisa turned round to get a better look.

Then she searched and realized that she could walk back along the trail without walking backwards.

"How silly of me," said Lisa.

The Bookworm just nodded. Lisa walked along, and the reader wriggled down the trail together with her. What a funny sight they made. Lisa was glad to be in the company of the Bookworm because it seemed much more sensible than the silly rabbits.

"So what are your favorite books?" asked the Bookworm.

"I love all types of books, but my favorite story has always been Alice in Wonderland," said Lisa. Then she looked a little sad.

"You don't seem to be happy." said the Bookworm.

"Well, you see, I wanted to understand what it felt like to be down a rabbit hole," said Lisa. Then Lisa explained to the Bookworm how she had fallen asleep under a tree, and somehow, a rabbit had hopped by, and she had followed the rabbit. Lisa carried on telling her story about the rabbits and rabbit school. It had been all extraordinary and fun initially; but it became silly and annoying on the other hand.

"I couldn't find my way home until a rabbit told me to walk backwards," said Lisa. The Bookworm giggled. Lisa could tell he understood how she felt. In any case, he was a Bookworm. He knew about exciting stories and imagination.

"I need to get home now," said Lisa, as she began to climb a crooked stairway. She was sure she could see a light at the top of the steps. The steps led up to some bushes. Lisa pushed the frontiers aside, and there, ahead of her, was the garden. Lisa was so relieved she flopped down on the grass and closed her eyes. She wanted to make sure that when she opened them again, she was already inside her home.

"Lisa, where are you?" called a voice. It was her Mom yelling from the kitchen. Lisa opened her eyes and blinked twice - there were no rabbits around. She breathed a sigh of relief. Then she saw her book lying on the grass. Lisa picked up the book, and she laughed aloud. Sitting on the book was a tiny inchworm. She watched it make some progress then let its body catch up, moving inch by inch.

"Hello, little worm," said Lisa as she gently took it over to the bushes and let it continue on a leaf.

"Who are you talking to?" asked her Mom. "Oh, just a little bookworm who helped me to find my way home," said Lisa. Her Mom laughed and muttered something about Lisa and her fantasy books.

The Duckling Story

A long time ago, on a small ranch, Mama Duck sat on her nest. "How will I know that my eggs will hatch?" she asked aloud. And she went on, "I stay here alone all day long! Nobody stays with me." But what can a mother duck do other than sitting patiently on her eggs to keep them warm until they are ready to hatch?

Finally, the eggs began to hatch. Individually, yellow ducklings ventured out of their shells. They shook their wings and yelled, "Quack, quack!"

"Look at you all!" said Mama Duck happily. "You are oh so charming!" "Quack, quack!" they said.

Mama Duck said, "Come and line up. We shall go right down to the lake for your first swim." She checked – one, two, three, four, and five. "Oh, dear!" she said. "I should have six ducklings!"

In any case, one large egg was still in the nest. "Well," said Mama Duck, "It seems that the big egg will take longer." So she needed to retake a seat on her nest and wait some more.

The following day, the giant egg began to hatch. Out came a little nestling. However, it was an odd-looking thing. This bird was very different to the others. He wasn't yellow at all - he was dull grey from his head to his feet. And he walked with a weird wobble.

One of the yellow ducklings pointed. "What is THAT? He cannot be one of us!" "I've never seen such an ugly duckling!" said another.

"How could you say something like that?" said Mama Duck in a stern voice. "You are just a day old! Your sibling hatched from the same nest as you. Now line up. We'll go to the pond for your first swim."

The other ducklings quacked, "Ugly! Ugly! Ugly!" The Odd Duck out didn't have a clue because other ducklings were shouting at him. He took the last spot in the line.

Each yellow duck bounced in the pond and swam behind Mama Duck. When it came time for him to swim, the Odd Duck out bounced in and began to paddle, as well. "Well, at least he can swim," Mama Duck said to herself.

When they left the water and began to play, the Odd Duckling tried to play together with his brothers and sisters.

They shouted, "Leave! We cannot play with you! You're ugly. And you walk strange!"

When Mama Duck was around, she wouldn't allow them to talk in this manner. "Be nice!" she would say. But she wasn't always around.

One time, one of the yellow ducklings said to the ugly duckling, "You know what? You'd do us a favor if you left us!" All of them began to quack, "Get out! Get out! Get out!"

"Why won't they let me stay here?" said the Odd Duckling to himself. He hung his head down low. "Ok, they're right. I should go."

That night, the ugly duckling flew over the farm fence. He flew until he arrived on the other side of the pond.

There he saw two grown-up ducks.

"Would I be able to please stay here for a while?" said the ugly duckling. "I haven't any other place else to go."

"Why should we care?" said one of the ducks. "Just don't hold us up."

"Woohoo! Woooooof!" an enormous hungry dog came tearing by suddenly, chasing the two ducks. They quickly flew up into the sky, and their feathers tumbled down on the bottom. The Odd Duckling froze in terror. The dog sniffed and sniffed at the duckling, then turned away. "I am too ugly even for the large hungry dog to eat," said the duckling with his head hung low.

The sky turned dark. Crack! Lightning flashed across the sky. Then, there was an enormous storm with massive downpours from the sky. In only minutes, the Odd Duckling was utterly soaked. Then, a chilly wind began to blow.

"Brrr!" he said together with his two wings held on the brink of his chest. "If only there were an area I could get dry." Just then, he saw a little light squinting in the distance of the woods. "Maybe it's somebody's hut?"

He flew to the entrance. "Quack?" said the Odd Duckling. The door of the hut squeaked open.

"What is that noise?" said an Old Woman, looking both ways. Her eyesight wasn't great. Then she looked down. "Oh, look, it's a duck!" She got the Odd Duckling and dropped him inside her hut. "You can stay here, but only if you lay eggs," she said.

A Tomcat and Hen came to play with the Odd Duckling. "Who do you think you are, coming in here and taking over our space by the fire!" said the Tomcat.

"Screech!" said the Hen. "I don't need another individual in this hut laying eggs."

"Try not to worry about that," said the Odd Duckling. "I am a baby duck."

"Then why are you here?" asked the Tomcat. "Did you not hear what the Old Woman said?" "Leave!" clacked the Hen.

"Get out! Get out!" yelled the Tomcat.

The door was still a little open, so our poor odd Duckling sneaked out of the doorway and back to the storm.

"Nobody wants me," said the Odd Duckling with a tear in his eye.

The storm ended. Soon, he found another lake. Staring into the water, he saw the reflection of a herd of giant white birds flying. He searched and couldn't believe what he saw. There were the most beautiful birds above him that he had ever seen! Their long white bodies and thin necks seemed to skim through the sky. He watched until the last bird had flown out of view.

He stayed at that lake without anyone else, and time passed. The leaves of the trees turned red and gold, and then the leaves fell to the bottom. Winter came, setting a sheet of white snow everywhere. The cold wind and the looming shadows made the Odd Duckling feel even more miserable. He needed to travel into the chilly, quiet lake to catch fish. But, it was getting harder to swim. The lake was starting to ice up. At one point, all he could do was to paddle in the water to prevent it from freezing around him and trapping him in the lake.

"I am so tired!" he sighed, paddling as hard as he could. The ice got thicker and moved closer to him.

Suddenly, two large hands picked him up. "You poor thing!" said a Farmer. He held the Odd Duckling by his thick fleece coat and took the bird to his home.

Never was a warm fireplace so welcome! For the remainder of the winter, the Farmer cared for the Odd Duckling. Then spring came. Tips of green covered the trees. Short, splendid blossoms sprung up from the ground. "It is best if you travel to the lake to swim again, as you were meant to," said the Farmer. He returned the duckling to the lake where he had discovered him and set him with care on the water.

"Gosh, I feel good," said the Duckling, fluttering his wings. "Why, I never felt nearly as good as I do right now!" He heard gentle sprinkling sounds behind him and rotated. A herd of these beautiful birds he had seen in the sky before arrived behind him on the water.

"Do not worry!" he said to them, holding out one wing, "I will go now. I won't bother you." An enormous fat tear rolled down his cheek. He turned to go away. When he opened his eyes, he saw a mirrored image in the water of one of these beautiful white birds. Why was it so close to him? He bounced back. What's more, the reflection bounced back, as well.

"What is this?" he said. He extended his neck, and the reflection of the gorgeous bird stretched its neck, as well.

"Why are you leaving so early?" said one of the gorgeous birds.

"Stay here, with us!" said another. "We'll be great friends."

Then, the bird who used to be the Odd Duckling understood what had happened! He was not an unsightly grey bird that wobbled when it walked.

Suddenly, all of the Swans fluttered their wings and took off into the sky. "Come with us," one called back. "Lead the group!" So he flapped his wings quickly and took his place ahead of the group. All of his new friends fluttered their wings behind him.

"Say!" he said, coasting and plunging through the sky as he sped on. "Who's an unsightly duckling now? Definitely, not me!"

Tina Feels Sad

Tina was about eight years old. She liked to jump rope, play jacks, color, ride her bike, and all of the other things that eight-year-olds like doing. She didn't just sit around and do nothing. She was always doing something. The best thing about Tina was that she was always smiling. There didn't appear to be anything that could ever bring Tina down. She woke up each morning filled with pep and energy, able to face the day.

Today was different. Tina woke up without a smile on her face. She didn't get out of bed as usual to embrace the day. A few hours later, she sluggishly left her bed and got dressed. She walked to the kitchen and poured herself a bowl of cereal.

She ate her cereal in silence. Mom came into the kitchen and kissed Tina on top of the top like she always did. Tina jerked her head, far away from her mom. "Leave me alone, Mom."

"Excuse me? What's wrong, Tina?" "Nothing, why?" she replied.

"Nothing? You're wearing the clothes you wore yesterday, you normally eat yogurt and fruit for breakfast, and you pulled far away from my kiss. Now, something is wrong."

"Nothing is wrong. I just want to be left alone."

Tina put her bowl in the sink and stomped off to her room. Tina usually would put her dirty dishes in the dishwasher then go outside to play. She would ride her bike to the park to play together with her friends. Today she just stomped to her room and slammed her door. Her Mom was worried about Tina. Something terrible must have happened for her bright, smiling female child to turn into a sullen grump. Her Mom decided to call her friends to find out if something had happened at school.

Tina's Mom got more and more worried as Tina refused to respond to her calls. Nobody could come up with anything that might explain why Tina was in such a nasty mood today. Tina's Dad came into the kitchen. "Good morning. Has Tina already gone to the park?"

"No, Tina is in her room."

"Is she sick?"

"Nope, she's in a bad mood." "Tina's in a bad mood?"

"Yep. She ate some cereal and told me to leave her alone. Afterward, she put her bowl in the sink, and stomped off to her room." "That's not our Tina."

"I know. I called her friends to see if something happened at college yesterday, but nobody could come up with anything." "Well, maybe we should just leave her alone. Children sometimes go through similar emotional changes as adults, except that they do not have the skills to process these emotions as we do. She won't even know what emotion she is experiencing. I've woken up repeatedly feeling sad or grumpy without having a reason." "Yeah, me, too, I just don't like seeing our sweet girl like this." "I know, but just give her a while. I'm sure she'll come round. If not, we'll talk together with her and see if we will help her understand what's happening."

Tina didn't know what she was feeling or why she was feeling this way. This was entirely new for her, and she couldn't understand how to manage it. She was out of her depth on this one. She began throwing toys, tearing pages out of her coloring books, and she threw all her clothes on the ground. In any case, she still didn't feel better. So, she thought she might begin feeling better if she rode her bike. She threw open her bedroom door so hard it slammed against the wall.

She stomped through the house and into the garage. "Tina, where are you going?"

"OUT!"

She met her Daddy outside. He was washing the car as Tina got her bike out of the garage. "Good morning, Tina. How are you today?"

"FINE!"

"Okay, are you going to the park?"

"I DON'T KNOW!"

"Okay, just take care."

Tina took off on her bike. She didn't know where she was going or what she was going to do. She didn't know what was happening inside. All she knew was that she wasn't herself, and it scared her. She felt like crying, screaming, and possibly punching something. She found herself in the park. She parked her bike beside the swings. There weren't any swings available and there was a line for the slide.

The climbing wall was full. Even all of the seesaws were occupied and it made her feel even worse.

She got back on her bike and started riding. She still didn't know what was happening or where she wanted to go, but she couldn't stay in the park anymore. She was riding along and found herself outside the library. "The library, maybe I can find peace there."

Tina went into the library and found her favorite book. She pulled it off the shelf and was close to sitting on a bean bag chair when another book caught her eye. She walked over to it. It was red with bright colors. It was a book about feelings.

"Maybe this will help me find out what's wrong."

Tina sat down with the book and started reading it. The various pictures and facial expressions were exciting to her, but she still couldn't find what she was feeling. A lot was going on inside her, and it was just too confusing. She decided to hire the books out and take them home. Maybe it was time to speak about it together with her parents. Tina took the books up to the Librarian. She placed the books on the desk, and the librarian picked up each book and scanned them into the PC. "Can I see your borrower's card, please?"

Tina didn't have her borrower's card with her. She didn't know she would be coming to the library when she left her house.

"I don't have it with me."

"I can't allow you to take these books without your borrower's card. I'm sorry." Tina felt like she was going to explode.

"My name is Tina Gouge. Can't you just look it up?"

"I'm sorry. I have to scan your card before you can take these books home. I can allow you to use the phone, and you can call your parents and ask them if they can bring you the card." Tina screamed. "I CAN'T TAKE IT ANYMORE!!!" Tina ran toward the toilet. On her way to the bathroom, she threw books, knocked over tables, and continued to scream.

The Librarian looked her name up on the PC and found her telephone number. She phoned her parents. "Hello, is this Tina Gouge's number?"

"Yes, ma'am. Who are you?"

"My name is Maxine Briggs, and I'm the librarian at the Broad Library. Tina is here. She was going to borrow some books but didn't have her card. Once I told her I couldn't let her take them home without scanning her card, she screamed and went toward the restrooms. On her way to the restroom, she threw books, turned over tables, and made an entire mess of the library. I could have called the police, but I thought I should let you know what was happening first. The library closes in one hour, and it's going to take me longer than that to get all this cleaned up."

"Ms. Briggs, I'm so sorry. Her Father and I are going to be there in a jiffy."

"Thank you,"

Tina was still in the bathroom, screaming and crying, when her parents arrived at the library. Tina's Dad immediately began helping the Librarian clear up the mess while Tina's Mom visited the restroom. Tina's Mom opened the restroom door and saw Tina sitting on the ground.

"Tina, honey, would you like to talk about what's bothering you?"

"That's the problem, Mom; I don't know what's bothering me."

"You made a mess in the library. I would like you to help Ms. Briggs and your Dad clean it up. Do you think you can do that?" Tina sniffled and nodded. "Yes."

"Wipe your face and blow your nose. Splash some cold water on your face and go back into the library." "Yes, Mom!"

Tina did as her Mom said. She walked back to the library and saw the mess she had made. She started crying again.

"Ms. Briggs, I'm sorry. I just don't know what's wrong with me today."

"That's okay. Everyone experiences different emotions. We just need to find out how to handle them." "But how are you able to handle them if you don't know what you're even feeling?"

"Were the books going to help you figure your emotions out?"

"Yes, I was reading through it but still couldn't find out what I am feeling. I wanted to take it home and ask my parents for help."

Tina's Dad reached into his pocket and pulled out his wallet. He handed his borrower's card to Ms Briggs. "Can I check those books out for Tina?"

Ms. Briggs smiled. "Yes, sir, you can. I'll get right to it."

Tina, with the assistance of her Mother, picked the last table up and placed it upright. She picked up all the books off the ground and put them on the table.

"Here are your books. Thanks for your help. I hope you'll find out what you are feeling, Tina." "Thanks."

Tina, alongside her parents, walked out into the Saturday sunlight.

"Are you going to ride your bike home, or do you want to place it in the truck?"

"I'll ride if that's okay."

"That's fine. We'll see you when you get back."

Tina's parents were waiting for her in the recreation room when she got home. Her Dad had the books in his lap.

"How do you want to try to do this?"

"I don't know. I just know that I would like it to go away."

"The very first thing we've got to do is see if we can find out what emotion you're experiencing. Are you able to tell me anything about what you've experienced today? Does it hurt anywhere?" Tina thought for a couple of minutes. "I've had a pain here." Tina pointed to the center of her chest. "Okay, anything else?"

"I start to feel hungry, but once I see food, I don't feel hungry anymore." Tina's Mom nodded her head. "That would explain breakfast."

"I also feel empty. Nothing that I like doing interested me this morning. I was so confused."

"That's understandable, honey. It seems to me that you simply could be experiencing the emotion of sadness."

"Did anything happen that might have made you feel sad?"

Tina frowned and thought. "Not that I can think of." "Have you lost anything?"

Again, Tina frowned. She ran to her room and grabbed her backpack. She unzipped the small front compartment. She reached inside and felt around. Her eyes crammed with tears. "It isn't there." She whispered. "What isn't there, honey?"

"The purple ring Aunt Joan gave me for my birthday."

"When did you realize it was missing?"

"I remember reaching into the pocket at college to offer June a pencil to use. I had a weird thought that my ring wasn't there, but I didn't think about it."

"While you slept, your brain processed that thought, and that is why you woke up feeling sad. You haven't ever experienced this emotion before, and you didn't know how to process it. You can't explode and tear things up when you don't understand what you're feeling."

"I know that now. What am I able to do? How do I make this feeling leave, and what if it comes back?" "Talk to your Mom or me.

I find that when I feel sad, if I can force myself to do something I enjoy doing, it makes me feel better.

I also ask friends or your Mom about what I'm feeling, and it makes me feel better." "I can do this. I wish I knew where my ring is."

"Have you searched for it?" "No."

"Maybe you'll find it once you clean your room."

Tina remembered she had torn her room up this morning. She closed her eyes. "I'm sorry, Mom, Dad, I'll go clean it now. Thanks for your help."

Tina hugged her parents and headed off to her room. Her parents followed her and helped her tidy up her room. Tina's Mom picked her clothes and put them back where they belonged. Tina's Dad helped her gather her toys and put them away. Her Dad brought the bin into her room for her to place all the torn pages in.

Tina was crawling around her floor, trying to get the papers scattered across the floor. Then she raised the bed sheet to find that there wasn't any more paper. Tina squealed and jumped up. "I found it!!" she screamed.

"Found what, honey?" Her Mom asked from the closet, turning to see what made her daughter scream with such excitement. Just then, Tina was putting the ring on her finger.

"My ring! I found my ring!"

"That's great, honey! Where did you find it?"

"I found it under my bed." "How could it have got there?"

"Well, I dropped my backpack the other night, and everything fell on the floor. I assumed I picked up everything, but I didn't. I'm just glad to have found it."

Tina's smile was back. Her entire face lit up. Her parents were happy to have their happy Tina back. It took one difficult day for Tina to find out that emotions are hard to work out, and it's good to speak to people about them. Sons and daughters have felt a bit like adults, and they learn the way to recognize what emotion they're feeling and the way to handle them. Tina learned that it's okay to ask for help when she needs it and speak to someone about her feelings to assist her through them.

The Mathematician Prince

In a faraway kingdom, there was a Prince who loved mathematics; He always wrote down scientific problems in his notebook and never used a computer.

One day, his father, King Tim, said, "My dear son, you should go out and make the most of our garden and get some fresh air. It is essential to have friends and relax by breathing in the outside air and meeting people. Please don't spend the whole day doing math in your room."

The Prince replied, "Well, I don't think I like that as much as I like mathematics."

The Prince barely knew his castle because he was always preoccupied with math problems and did not look around. He had never seen the world outside his room, the number of hallways and doors, and he did not know which door led to the back garden. Suddenly he saw a large wooden door at the end of a corridor. He wondered what it could be. Then the door opened.

But it wasn't the right door. The Prince entered a dark room and could not see anything. After taking two steps, he heard a voice say, "You have entered the most dangerous room in history. Three questions must be answered to get out. If you make a mistake, you will never see sunlight again. The first question is: What is 489 multiplied by 360?"

"176,040!" the Prince responded.

"Correct!" The voice shouted, "You can continue."

The Prince continued walking through the room, taking in everything around him until he found himself on a high cliff with no way out. The voice said:

"Now I have three questions for you, a platform will appear for each one, and then you can cross the cliff to the other side, but if you miss one of them, the platform will disappear, and you will fall into a deep abyss and get eaten by snakes and crocodiles. The first question is ... what is 92 divided by 2 minus 4 divided by 1 over 5 minus 8 over 3?"

The Prince thought about it before responding. Three seconds later, the prince said, "Two!"

"You're right! Here's the first platform."

The young Prince obeyed and the voice then said: "The next question: What is 64 divided by 8 plus 3 divided by 2 plus 6 divided by 5 plus 9 divided by 3?"

The Prince said: "61," confidently.

"Correct!" The voice said and added, "Walk to the next platform and pay attention to the third question: What is

43,126 multiplied by 89? You only have 5 seconds to respond. "

The Prince knew the question was complicated and thought it would take more than 5 seconds. He put in an extraordinary effort and cried three-thousandths of a second before the time was up:

"3838214!!!"...

"Correct!" The voice said, "Keep going; you only have one question left."

The Prince continued walking down the dark corridors, aware of everything around him. Suddenly, he saw a light shining at the end of the corridor coming from the door, so the Prince ran to the door, but it quickly closed and the alarms went off. The voice spoke again: "This is the last question that must be answered before these walls close and turn you into a human pie! The question is: If you add 18 to a number and then subtract 53 and the result is multiplied by 3, the final score is 195. What is the first number?"

The Prince had never encountered such a complex mathematical problem. He had covered several topics, but nothing like this. His nerves clung to him, and he saw the sharp walls approaching meaning the end of his life, and he could not focus on the answer to the question.

There was only an inch of space left before the Prince of Mathematics would be crushed and start his long journey to Heaven. Out of nowhere, it occurred to him that the correct answer is: "100, number 100!" The Prince cried out.

Then the walls stopped, the Prince's life had been saved. He ran to the door where his father had stopped. King Tim said: "What are you doing?"

The Prince said, "I was misled searching for the garden." "I got in by mistake. But it was fun; I nearly died, but I knew the correct answer before the walls crushed me."

"Boy," said the man, "If you don't spend the whole day in your room locked in math, the worst outcome will happen. I'm sorry for trying to isolate you from this action. Now, you can keep doing what you've been doing if you want to."

His son said, "Yes, Dad, I will continue what I was doing: Find the path to the park. I've been thinking, and I think the best thing is to get out and get some fresh air. Mathematics is also suitable for people in everyday life, so you don't have to stop thinking about it, even if it's the most stressful topic in school. But staying all day locked up in my room away from the world to do just one thing is also unacceptable. I know it's a good idea to go out and spend time with other people, especially those of my age. That is why, from now on and for the foreseeable future, I will be thinking and having fun at the same time. I won't be locked up all day without talking to anyone. I will dedicate the first hours of the day to my schooling, and after doing my homework, then I'll go out to play with my new friends. Thank you, Dad!" The Prince was never alone in his room again. When he got home from school, he did his homework and then went out to play with his friends.

The Mouse Finds A Snack

When winter comes, finding a snack is often hard for a mouse.

In the winter, the snow falls and covers everything with majestic thick, icy blankets.

Usually, mice would feed on grains and tiny pieces of food over the summer and would hide them in their burrow so that they could eat all winter long.

That is what Mr. Mouse had been doing all summer, a bit like the other mice in his family had.

Mr. Mouse and his wife, Mrs. Mouse, and their children Little Mouse and Baby Mouse had spent the entire summer preparing a burrow filled with food for themselves.

They had collected grains, seeds, and little chunks of fruits that they might easily deduce to their burrow and conceal away in their nest to eat at a later date.

They took care never to eat an excessive amount to ensure that there would be enough food for them to enjoy all winter long.

As they were gathering their food all summer, Mrs. Mouse was bound to store them properly. She organized each sort of food separately and made sure they could eat them in the winter.

She sorted out pieces that weren't good and put them far away from their hearty food pile. All summer, Mrs. Mouse made it her mission to see that her family would have a tidy and delicious food pile to eat from as the world around them grew colder.

Until recently, everything was going as planned.

Their food storage was whole and healthy, their bellies were growing nice and fat for the cold winter, and their burrow was looking cozy. They thought that they had everything mapped out.

Then, one day, they heard a loud sound above the ground.

Terrified, they ran out of their burrow to find out what had happened.

Outside, they saw a massive machine moving toward them, so they hurried away as fast as they could. They hurried away just in time for an enormous backhoe to scoop away where their burrow had been, scooping away their entire home and food pile at the same time. Before they knew it, everything that they had worked on was gone in a moment, and they had no idea what to do now.

As they watched their home get taken away, Mrs. Mouse, Little Mouse, and Baby Mouse cried. Mr. Mouse stood by, sad and feeling helpless that he couldn't help his Family.

The family watched for hours as the dozers and backhoes destroyed their entire home and, therefore, the homes of all their mice friends. Before they knew it, they were all homeless, and there was nothing they could do.

The food that each of the mice had gathered all summer long was gone, and they barely had enough time left to repair the mess that was made.

Many of Mr. and Mrs. Mouse's friends were frozen with fear and could do nothing. They sat by the bottom of the trees a brief distance far away from the machinery and watched as everything they had ever known disappeared before their very eyes.

Other friends gathered up their children and left to pursue a new life elsewhere, knowing that there was nothing they could do to repair what had happened.

They would find another place with new food and new friends to play with and hope they have enough time to recover what they had lost.

Others still stayed by the edge of the forest and dug new burrows not too far away from the old ones, unwilling to go away from their home and leave their forest behind.

They appeared to trust that these big machines wouldn't come to take away more land, so they stayed close.

Mr. Mouse, Mrs. Mouse, Little Mouse, and Baby Mouse had no idea what they would do.

Mr. Mouse knew he needed to come up with an idea as quickly as possible, but he couldn't seem to wrap his mind around what had happened or around what they ought to do about it. The Mouse family wandered the forest for a short time, trying to develop a relocation plan. As time went by, they realized it was getting colder, and they barely had enough food for them to feast on.

If they were to create a new food stash by winter, they would almost certainly fail, and there would be no way that they would have enough for all of them.

Mr. Mouse thought it was best to leave behind what was left of their food to their friends who were staying close to their old homes. He decided that the Mouse family would travel further away from the forest and find something else. The Mouse family travelled far away, leaving everything behind.

They travelled through the forest, around a swamp, and into a populated area where people lived.

Mrs. Mouse grew fearful, as she had heard bad things about the urban areas and was scared for her family. She worried that if they stayed near people, they might be shooed away, or worse.

Mr. Mouse was certain, however, that this could be their chance to get enough food to make it through winter, so he insisted that they venture on and find an area to make a hideout.

The Mouse family moved carefully past restaurants, pedestrians, and all kinds of big scary animals that lived in the city.

They hid under grates when birds flew by, and they scurried behind dumpsters when angry restaurant owners came out with their bags filled with garbage.

Each time one would throw a bag into the trash, all of the town mice and rats would begin to eat the leftover food in the garbage bags.

Mr. Mouse knew that he and his family couldn't compete with them because the city mice and rats were all much bigger than they were. They continued down allies and across yards until they found a little neighborhood that appeared to be reasonably quiet.

Despite a few mice in the area, there appeared to be no birds, cats, or more giant rats on sight. Instead, it seemed as if Mr. Mouse and his family were pretty alone in this area. They continued their task of finding a new home.

As they continued walking, the Mouse family smelt something so delightful that it made all four of them stop in their tracks and turn their noses up towards the scent.

They had never smelt something so delightful before, and they couldn't help themselves but follow the smell to find out where it was coming from.

They were already so hungry and had come this far and they weren't sure about where they might find food in such an area. So, they trusted their noses and followed the smell. They followed the scent through a yard, under a gate, across a garden, and up to the rear patio of a house. The house seemed normal, at least to them.

But inside, the house was glowing with warm yellow lights and smelt of something so tasty that their bellies rumbled.

Determined to get a snack for his family, Mr. Mouse went inside to have a peek while Mrs. Mouse, Little Mouse, and Baby Mouse waited on the patio.

When he got inside, Mr. Mouse immediately saw where the smell was coming from. On the counter, a freshly baked loaf of bread was resting by the oven.

The smell was so delightful that Mr. Mouse almost didn't notice when someone made his way into the kitchen towards the bread. Before anyone saw him, he hurried under the counter and hid far away from the human. When he thought it was safe, he carefully peeked out from his hiding spot and watched a little older lady cutting the bread as she talked to her husband in the other room. Mr. Mouse could see that small crumbs would fall on the counter every time she cut the bread.

He hoped she would go away them there so he could quickly grab some for his family. The woman did even better than that.

After she finished cutting the bread, the woman slathered a couple of slices in butter and put the remainder away in the cupboard.

Then, she used the rear of her hand to brush all of the crumbs off the counter and straight on the ground in front of

Mr. Mouse! He was so delighted for such a special treat that he silently thanked the woman as she walked out of the kitchen.

When she was gone, Mr. Mouse picked up all of the crumbs in his cheeks and took as much as he could outside for the Family.

The Mouse family sat on the patio of this tiny house glowing yellow, eating breadcrumbs and staying warm in the heat that lightly radiated from the door.

As they did, they talked about what they might do next so that they could live comfortably through the winter.

Mr. and Mrs. Mouse decided that they might find somewhere near the house to stay comfortable and warm and have access to fresh breadcrumbs whenever they wanted.

He also suggested that perhaps many other homes in the neighborhood would have something yummy for them to eat.

When they were done eating, they found a tiny hole in the patio which led to a warm space directly under the older lady's house. Surprisingly, nobody had made this their home yet, so the Mouse family officially moved in.

They spent the rest of the winter getting fresh food directly from the older lady's house and every one of her neighbors.

They enjoyed everything from breadcrumbs to muffin crumbs and even small pieces of cheese when they were lucky.

They had never been so happy, and they felt so thankful that they found such an exquisite home before the cold winter came.

Under that patio, the Mouse family lived happily ever after.

Conclusion

Thank you again for reading – "***Bedtime stories for kids.***"

It's also vital for child development that you read to your children, and bedtime is one of the most convenient times in a parent's busy day for this. Reading to your children benefits them in several ways.

When you read bedtime stories to your child, you're providing him with far more than brief entertainment. Just by reading out loud, you're preparing your child for the longer term by helping them develop skills and character traits which will be helpful throughout their lifetime.

Parents and youngsters strengthen their bonds as they share this quiet activity. It is often a beloved tradition that has long been passed down from one generation to another. It allows memories to be created, which will be treasured forever.

From a purely functional standpoint, reading out loud to children may be practical and enjoyable in helping kids relax and unwind before sleep. Many parents find that this brief respite from the cares and worries of life also helps them to relax and relieves much of their everyday stress.

Reading stories is a sure way to assist your child in developing a much larger and better grasp of English language vocabulary, which can help improve their speaking and writing.

Printed in Great Britain
by Amazon